SMALL GROUP DISCUSSION TOPICS

FOR KOREAN TEENAGERS

BY JACK MARTIRE

FOURTH EDITION

TOPICS IMPORTANT TO KOREAN TEENAGERS
PRESENTED IN CONVERSATIONAL
NORTH AMERICAN ENGLISH

PNU PRESS WWW.SGDT.NET

SMALL GROUP DISCUSSION TOPICS
FOR KOREAN TEENAGERS

by Jack Martire

Published by Pusan National University Press

First Edition: January 1998
Second Printing: April 1999
Third Printing: September 1999
Fourth Printing: October 2000
Fifth Printing: July 2001
Sixth Printing: March 2002
Seventh Printing: March 2003
Second Edition: September 2004
Eighth Printing: November 2004
Ninth Printing: January 2006
Tenth Printing: August 2006
Third Edition: September 2007
Eleventh Printing: October 2007
Fourth Edition: May 2010
Twelfth printing : March 2013

For information address: Pusan National University Press
Busandaehangro 63 beon-gil 2, Geumjeong-gu, Busan 609-735
Republic of Korea(KR)
Tel: (8251) 510-1932
Fax: (8251) 512-7812

Questions or comments pertaining to the contents should be addressed to the author
via email at: jack@sgdt.net

Price : 12,000 won

ISBN 978-89-7316-346-5 03740
Reg. No. 11-2, Sept. 10, 1992

Printed in the Republic of Korea

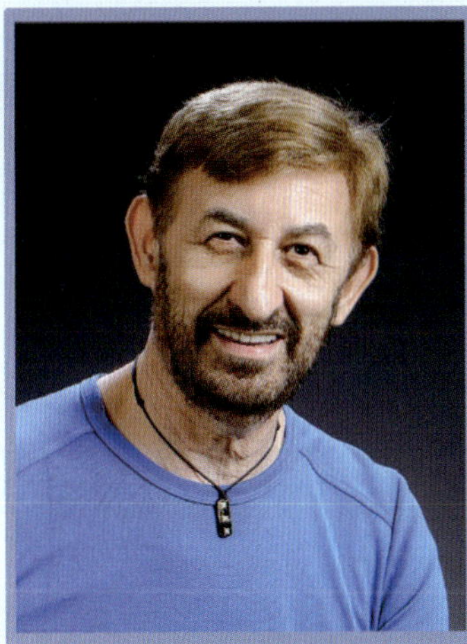

Jack Martire holds an M.Ed. in English education from Pennsylvania State University and has pursued additional graduate studies in International Affairs and Asian languages at universities and language centers in the USA, Japan and Thailand. He has studied 9 European and Asian languages but considers himself the most proficient in Japanese, Korean, and Thai.

He taught high school English for the US Department of Defense in Germany and Japan for 4 years and served as a US Customs inspector on the US/Canadian border while a graduate student majoring in International Affairs at the University of Pittsburgh. However, the bulk of his professional career has been spent teaching and directing English language programs in Japan and Korea. Honolulu, Hawaii is home, but he currently resides in Bangkok, Thailand, where he is working on a Thai version of SGDT.

Prof. Martire began his ESL teaching career in Japan, where he taught English at a private high school in Hitachi for 4 years while simultaneously operating his own English conversation school in nearby Mito. In 1980 he joined the staff of a private university in Busan and taught at a number of public and private universities including PNU and the Korea Maritime University. He joined the staff of the foreign language institute at Sogang University in 1990, the same year he published the first edition of Small Group Discussion Topics for Korean Students. He later served as director of the English language training program for the Kolon Corporation Training Center in Yongin until 1998.

Prof. Martire believes that fluency is best acquired not through textbook dialogues, memorization, and classroom drills with which students cannot identify but through situations requiring practical use of the language, similar to the way that babies learn to talk. Asked to discuss subjects with which they are already familiar, students tend to focus on the content of their discussions and lose sight of the fact that they are first and foremost using a foreign language.

SCHOOL AND LEARNING

FAMILY AND FRIENDS

ALL ABOUT KOREA

SMALL GROUP DISCUSSION TOPICS FOR KOREAN TEENAGERS

OUR WORLD

HIGH TECH

SPECIAL INTERESTS

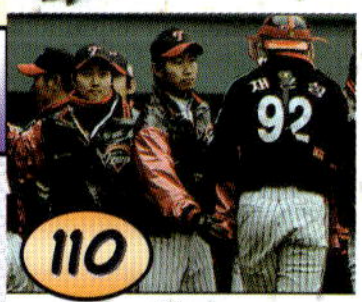

APPENDIX

INTRODUCTION

CHANGING TIMES

When first published in 1998 Small Group Discussion Topics for Korean High School students was the first of its kind. High school students in Korea had always been too preoccupied with passing the notoriously competitive college entrance exam to spend any time learning English conversation.

The exam emphasized reading comprehension and written translation, so any high school student who spent time learning to actually speak English risked being accused of wasting time. As crazy as that sounds, that's how bad the state of English education in Korea was until the mid-1990s.

The era of globalization changed everything. Today Koreans realize that the prosperity of their country depends not only on the industriousness, creativity, and determination of the people but also on the country's ability to play a role in the global marketplace. In the reality of today's world, how well a country can perform that role depends in great part on the ability of its people to communicate in English, the international language of business.

AN EDUCATION FIRST

In a move to equip the next generation of Koreans with English language abilities that previous generations lacked, Korean educators in 1995 broke with decades-old tradition and moved the beginning of English instruction down from the middle school to the 3rd grade of elementary school. The result of this remarkable change is that today it is not only acceptable for young children to be learning English, but it is thought that parents who do not enroll their children in English conversation classes are probably gambling with their children's futures. That's quite a reversal from just half a generation ago.

Until the first edition of this book was printed in 1998 all English conversation materials available in Korea were designed for adult learners. No conversation books with teenagers in mind had ever appeared on Korean bookstore shelves. *SGDT for Korean H.S. Students* was the first.

THE TOPICS

Most of the topics in this book focus on issues that affect teenagers in their daily lives—studying and taking tests, choosing friends, and the pains and pressures of just being an adolescent. No subjects are shunned, especially not those that traditional-minded Korean educators might consider too provocative to include in a textbook for high school kids, topics like teenage sex, suicides, school violence, gangs, and smoking, all of which have become major headaches for contemporary Korean society.

While topics like these were not issues a generation ago, they affect the lives of every Korean teenager today and therefore cannot ignored. While some teachers educated a few decades ago might feel uncomfortable discussing topics related to sex with their students, it's a safe bet that most students won't feel the same.

THE READINGS

The readings that introduce the topics are written in plain and simple conversational North American English with some colloquial expressions thrown in. Some sentences may not pass the test of grammatical excellence, but they sound the way people talk.

The whole point is to expose students to spoken English, the kind not normally found in books or magazines, so some bending of the rules is inevitable. Students are also exposed to many alternative word usages and new expressions such as "to party" or "to text" (on a cell phone) that didn't even exist a few years ago.

PRACTICE EXERCISES

At the end of each reading is a brief Practice section that focuses on vocabulary or word usages contained in the article. Students may be asked to make new sentences, fit vocabulary into sentences, or write new sentences. Answers to all of the exercises are found in the Answers section in the Appendix at the back of the book.

KOREAN TRANSLATIONS

To ensure correct understanding, translations of all of the readings and discussion questions are printed in the Appendix at the back of the book. The translations were done by Jason Shin, a Korean national and 2005 Phi Beta Kappa graduate of Honolulu's Hawaii Pacific University. Mr. Shin is currently employed by a Fortune 500 company and resides in Laurel, MD, a suburb of Washington, D.C.

SGDT.NET

In this book I have tried to provide interesting content that young students will find useful and from which they can learn and improve their English conversation ability. Since some of the topics are related to current conditions that can suddenly change, the SGDT series has its own website, www.sgdt.net, where updates and supplementary material pertaining to events in Korea can be posted.

My purpose in creating the SGDT series was to help Korean students understand that English is more than a subject to study in school that it really is a living language and a tool for communication and for getting things done in the real world. It is my sincere hope that students come away with that sense after studying with this book, a somewhat radical departure from past methods of study.

Jack Martire,
May 2010

HOW TO USE THIS BOOK

PROCEDURE

The material in this book can be used in a variety of ways, depending on the ability level of the students. While the book was designed to be used with small groups of students, thus the title "Small Group Discussion Topics", in cases where the English ability of students is not high enough for students to carry on discussions on their own, such as with middle school students, it can be used with an entire class of students with the instructor as group leader. Ideally, of course, the class would be broken up into smaller groups of 5 to 7 students with each group having its own discussion leader.

If the ability level is such that the class can be broken up, it's important to ensure that each group contains students of varying levels of ability rather than have students choose their own groups. If allowed to choose, students will choose their friends, who are likely to be at the same ability level, increasing the possibility that some groups will contain all of the best students while other groups contain students whose ability level is not good enough to hold a discussion.

PARTICIPATION

At the end of each unit is a list of 8 to 10 discussion questions. These are not reading comprehension questions but instead are questions which ask students to give their opinions about what they have read. To respond to the questions students will have to be familiar with the terms used in the reading because they may have to use those words to respond properly. It is expected that each question be answered by each student, rather than have just one student respond to a question and then move on to the next question and another student.

By having each student respond to each question, differences of opinion occur, and this is ideal. When disagreeing, students are forced to defend their own points of view. Needless to say, students should be encouraged to converse only in the target language and avoid using Korean as much as possible.

PREPARATION

Before discussions can be held it is important that students understand the article preceding the questions. They should also run through the brief exercise in the Practice section for practice using some of the vocabulary in the reading. While the students are not asked to repeat the content of the readings in their answers, they still need to understand the content.

The instructor can choose either to read the article to the students or have students take turns reading paragraphs, after which the instructor allows students to ask questions about passages they aren't sure of. The point is to make sure that students understand the content of the reading before being broken into small groups to hold their discussions.

INSTRUCTOR'S ROLE

Once the students have been divided into small groups the instructor in charge should play the role of observer or occasional participant in the discussions. He or she should move around from group to group, interjecting a question or comment from time to time in order to stimulate discussion but never assuming a leading role. Students will be all too willing to let the teacher take over and do all of the talking, but that shouldn't be allowed to happen.

While making the rounds, teachers may be tempted to correct students' ungrammatical sentences, but they should refrain from cutting in. The only exception is if and when a student is having a hard time pronouncing a word or phrase, in which case the teacher should assist. But for the most part, making on-spot corrections is a no-win situation since it shatters the momentum that the students had going before the interruption, and it makes students afraid to open their mouths for fear they will say something wrong. All that really matters is that students are practicing English; the time for corrections will come later.

WRAP-UP SESSION

When the instructor senses that the topic has been sufficiently discussed but before a lull sets in, it is time to dissolve the groups and rejoin the class for another 10 minute session. The purpose of this wrap-up session is to summarize the important points that came out during the discussions. During this session students should be given a chance to restate for the whole class some of the opinions they expressed in their small groups. This is the time for teachers to make grammatical or other corrections.

Experience has shown that if the above procedures are followed, high school students with moderate ability can carry on a discussion for 25 or 30 minutes. However, this is just an estimate, since depending on the topic, the student level of proficiency, and the degree of interest in the topic, the time covered will vary quite a bit.

UNIT 1 HIGH SCHOOL LIFE

KOREA VS. USA

Going to high school in the U.S.A. is a lot different from going to high school in Korea. Of course, some things are the same—classrooms, books, teachers, and tests. But that's where the similarities end.

Getting to school For one thing, most Korean high school students go to school by subway or public bus, but most American students either ride yellow school buses or drive cars to school. Most high schools in the U.S. even have parking lots for students to park their cars.

Books and things Korean students carry heavy book bags containing all of their books, pens, and other personal belongings. American students leave most of their books and other things inside their school lockers. They take home only the books they will need to do their homework.

Uniforms Korean students wear uniforms, but most American students don't. Only the few students who go to private schools wear uniforms.

HARD WORDS

- **that's...end**: Everything else is different
- **personal belongings**: such as hairbrushes, tissues, notebooks, etc.
- **locker**: a closet that can be locked, such as the ones used by students at school
- **private schools**: schools that are not paid for with taxes

A SCHOOL

A LOCKER

Part-time jobs Most Korean high school students cannot imagine it, but in the U.S. it is normal for teenagers to have part-time jobs. They work at fast food restaurants, car washes, or supermarkets. Americans think that teenagers who earn their own spending money learn the value of money better than teenagers who just take money from their parents.

Social life American students have more chances to socialize with members of the opposite sex at parties and on field trips than Korean students do. American boys and girls study together in the same classrooms, but in Korea they each study in separate classrooms.

Also, American high schools have dances every weekend, but Korean schools don't.

School Curriculum. In both the USA and Korea a wide range of regular subjects like mathematics, history, biology, foreign languages, art, and music are taught.

But American schools teach at least one subject that Korean students never learn—driver education. The USA is a big country and everybody has to know how to drive a car. That's why American high school students learn how to drive when they're just 16 years old.

A FIELD TRIP

LEARNING TO DRIVE AT AGE 16

HARD WORDS

- **spending money**: money to buy personal items
- **learn...money**: They learn to spend money wisely
- **socialize**: to meet with other students, make new friends
- **field trips**: school study trips
- **wide range**: many different kinds

Classes American kids have homerooms, the same as Korean students do, but they don't stay with the same students all day long. Even though they are in the same homeroom, the students don't all study the same subjects. Just like college students, they have different classmates in each class.

Sports Korean schools have the same sports teams, but there is a bigger emphasis on sports in American schools. At right is the long list of sports played at a typical American high school.

Fall Sports

CROSS COUNTRY
GIRLS' TENNIS
FOOTBALL
GIRL'S SOCCER
VOLLEYBALL

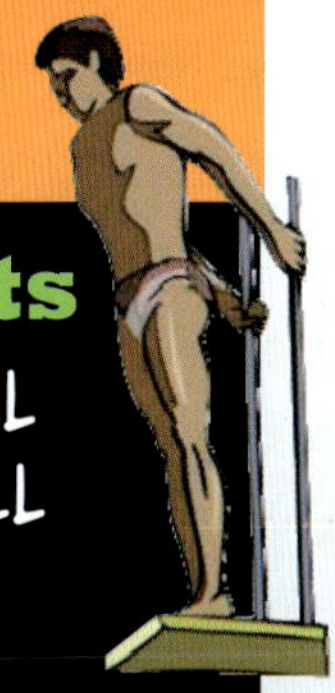

Winter Sports

BOY'S BASKETBALL
GIRL'S BASKETBALL
SWIMMING
WRESTLING

Spring Sports

BASEBALL
BOYS' SOCCER
BOYS' TENNIS
TRACK AND FIELD

Computer classes Almost every American high school offers courses in computer education. Many schools even offer online courses so that students can learn from home.

HARD WORDS

- **a...emphasis**: More time is spent on sports
- **typical**: average, normal, usual
- **Cross Country**: marathon running (long distance running)
- **Track and Field**: short distance running, jumping, javelin throw, discus, field sports
- **online course**: A class that is taught over the Internet

PRACTICE

MAKE NEW SENTENCES USING THE WORDS IN ORANGE.

...personal belongings

1. She...closet
2. I...book bag
3. You...room

HE KEEPS ALL HIS PERSONAL BELONGINGS IN HIS LOCKER.

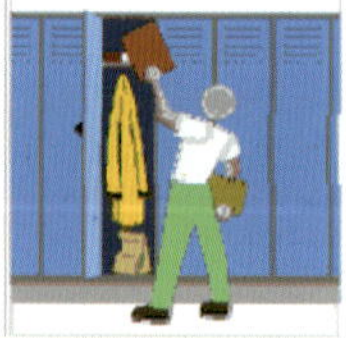

...to socialize

4. We...on weekends?
5. My sister...at church
6. He...at club meetings?

THEY SOCIALIZE AT PARTIES AND ON FIELD TRIPS.

ANSWERS ON PAGE 122

DISCUSS

1. Tell about your school.
   a. Is your school coeducational or same-sex (all boys or all girls)?
   b. Are the classes coeducational or same sex?
   c. How many classrooms are there, how many students per class?
   d. What is your favorite time of day at school? Tell why.
2. In the USA the summer break is 3 months long, but the winter break is just 2 weeks. When are your breaks in Korea and how long are they? Which schedule do you like better—USA's or Korea's? Why?
3. Is it a good idea for high school students to have part-time jobs? Why or why not? If you had a part-tine job, what kind of job would you like to have and why?
4. Is it a good idea for high school students to drive cars? Why or why not? What age is the best age to learn to drive a car? Tell why you think so.

5. Name the sports that are played at your school. Do you play any sport, and if so, which sport?
6. What do you think of having dances in high school? Would you like to have dances at your school? Why or why not?
7. Does your school teach computer classes? If so, are all students required to take the class? Are any classes taught over the Internet?
8. Are there any clubs at your school? Do you belong to a club? If so, which one? How often do you meet and what do you do at the meetings?
9. What is your favorite subject at school? Why do you like that subject?

UNIT 2 COEDUCATION

COED VS SAME-SEX

Korean elementary schools are coeducational, but most middle and high schools are not. It's true that boys and girls go to the same schools, but they learn in separate, same-sex classrooms. This means that Korean schools are coeducational but the classes are not.

Many Korean students envy students in the U.S. and other western countries where both sexes study together. They think that they would learn better if they could study with members of the opposite sex. Most Korean teachers and parents disagree.

Kissing in school Korean teachers who like the present system say that they don't need the problems that are caused by coeducation. One of these problems is teenage romance. Korean students might be shocked if they went to a school in an English-speaking country. They would probably see boys and girls hugging, and even kissing in school.

HIGH SCHOOL KIDS KISSING AT SCHOOL

HARD WORDS

- **same-sex**: all boys or all girls
- **to envy**: They want to have and do the same things
- **opposite sex**: males and females are opposite sexes
- **hugging:** put their arms around each other

Distraction. Because of the distraction that is caused by having members of the opposite sex in the classroom, some school districts in the U.S. are now trying all-boys' and all-girls' schools. They hope that students will be able to learn better. The idea seems to be working. Teachers in school districts where boys and girls are separated say that students study and learn better.

Unequal education. But the idea of sending boys and girls to separate schools is a radical idea in the U.S. It goes against tradition. Also, some people are afraid that if boys and girls are sent to different schools the education that the students receive may not be equal.

The idea behind coeducation is to make sure that girls get the same quality of education that boys receive. Many countries have laws saying that boys and girls must study together in the same classrooms in all public schools.

AN AMERICAN HIGH SCHOOL

A CO-ED CLASS

HARD WORDS

- **distraction**: They can't study hard because they are always thinking about their girlfriend or boyfriend
- **radical**: very different, not expected, shocking
- **goes...tradition:** is different from what is normal
- **(be) equal:** have the same quality, neither one is better than the other
- **public schools**: paid for with tax money

PRACTICE

MAKE NEW SENTENCES USING THE WORDS IN ORANGE.

...to envy 1. She...so smart. 2. They...so rich. 3. He...so handsome.	I ENVY HIM FOR BEING SUCH A GREAT SWIMMER. 
...to be equal 4. love...their mother 5. enjoyment...singing 6. money...their father	 THE HOMEWORK THEY GET FROM THEIR TEACHER IS EQUAL.

ANSWERS ON PAGE 122

DISCUSS

1. What do you think of coeducation in Korean schools? Tell why you think so.
   a. Boys and girls should study in the same classroom.
   b. It's better for boys and girls to study in different classrooms.

2. Do you agree that putting boys and girls in the same classroom makes students fall in love more? Tell why you think so.

3. Does putting boys and girls in the same classroom make it easier or harder to learn? Tell why you think so.
   a. It is harder to learn.
   b. It is easier to learn.
   c. It doesn't make any difference—not harder, and not easier.

4. If girls are in separate classrooms will the teachers teach them the same way that they teach boys, or will they teach the boys better? Tell why you think so.

5. Should boys and girls get equal education, or should boys get a better education than the girls? Tell why you think so.

6. Why have Korean schools always been same-sex in the past? Why have they taught boys separately from girls? Why do boys and girls still learn in separate classrooms?

7. Same-sex American schools say that their students learn better than students in coeducational schools. Doesn't that mean that same-sex education is better? Why or why not?

8. Should students be allowed to kiss and hug their boyfriends or girlfriends at school? Why or why not? Can it be stopped? If so, how?

UNIT 3 LEARNING ENGLISH

WHY STUDY ENGLISH?

Just a few years ago Korean students studied English only in middle school and high school. They studied mostly written English. They learned how to read and write English, but they didn't learn how to speak it.

Entrance Exam. The reason was that they had to prepare for the difficult college entrance exam. They weren't tested on their ability to speak English. They just had to know English grammar and how to read it.

Changing times But times have changed. Today even pre-schoolers (3 or 4 years old) are learning English. They're learning the ABCs and basic English conversation. When they graduate from high school they'll probably be able to have conversations in English with native speakers.

LITTLE KIDS ARE ALSO LEARNING ENGLISH

HARD WORDS

- **written English**: The English sentences in books and magazines are different from "spoken English"
- **weren't...on**: They were no questions on the test about it
- **times...changed**: Things are different today
- **native speakers**: people who learn English from when they are born

Today learning English is more important than ever before. Many Korean companies are selling their products in foreign countries, so Korean businessmen have to speak English well. That's why English conversation is now being taught beginning in the 3rd grade of elementary school.

Learning aids. Learning a language is not the same today as it was 15 or 20 years ago. Now we have computer software and other electronic learning tools that make learning English easy and fun. It is also possible to learn English from Internet websites. A lot of the software looks like computer games, so students enjoy studying more. Most kids would rather learn English from a computer than from a book.

Nobody can become fluent in English without speaking and listening practice. For that reason most high schools have English clubs where students can practice speaking English with their friends.

LEARNING ENGLISH ON COMPUTERS IS FUN AND GAMES.

HARD WORDS

- **3rd grade**: students are 8 or 9 years old
- **elementary school**: Grades 1 to 6 (students from 7 to 12 years old)
- **software**: computer programs that you can buy on CDs
- **electronic...tools**: computers, tape recorders, DVD players
- **(be) fluent**: be able to speak fast like a native speaker

PRACTICE

MAKE NEW SENTENCES USING THE WORDS IN BLUE AND GREEN.

...to prepare for... 1. I... party all week. 2. We...trip... a month. 3. They...meeting...all day.	WE PREPARED FOR THE TEST BY STUDYING HARD. 
...to resemble 4. She...her mother. 5. I...my father. 6. My sister...our aunt Susan	 HIS LITTLE BROTHER RESEMBLES THEIR DAD.

ANSWERS ON PAGE 122

DISCUSS

1. What do you think of teaching English to small children? Tell why you think so.
   a. It's a good idea. Better to start when very young.
   b. Little kids don't need to learn English; Korean is enough.
2. How do you feel about learning English? Tell why you think so.
   a. I like learning English very much.
   b. I don't like learning English because it's too difficult.
   c. I don't like to study English, but I like to speak it.
3. What's the main reason why you are studying English now?
   a. I enjoy it.
   b. I have to pass the college entrance exam.
   c. I will need English to get a good job in the future.
   d. I will need English to travel to foreign countries.
4. Have you ever used any computer software to learn English? If so, how was it? Do you enjoy learning English on a computer? Why or why not?
5. Why is each of these a good way to learn English?
   a. Watch TV programs and movies in English.
   b. Practice speaking English with native speakers.
   c. Use English conversation computer software.
6. Is it important to be a member of an English club at school? Does your school have an English club, and if so, are you a member? Why or why not?
7. Is it possible to become a good speaker of English without going to school in an English-speaking country? Why or why not?

UNIT 4 STUDYING FOR TESTS

TOO MANY EXAMS

Taking tests is a way of life for Koreans. There seems to be no end to the tests that they have to take.

High school entrance Until 1997, the first important examination that Korean students had to take was the high school entrance exam. All 9th grade students had to take the test. The test score decided which high school a student would attend. That test was dropped in 1998.

College entrance A big test that students still worry about is the *suneung*, or college entrance exam. Every high school senior who wants to go to college has to take this test. The score is used to decide which university the student will attend. Students who want to attend a prestigious university in Seoul have to get a very high score on this test.

PRESTIGIOUS YONSEI UNIVERSITY IN SEOUL.

HARD WORDS

- **(be) a...life:** something that they do all the time, a normal part of their life
- **ninth-grade:** the third year of middle school
- **senior:** a student in the last year of school
- **prestigious:** highly respected, thought to be one of the best

Special license tests The test-taking doesn't stop even after a student gets into a college or university. Before a senior can get a job he or she may have to take a *cha-kyok-cheung*, which is a test for a special license.

Then, even after getting a job with a company, there are periodic promotion tests. The scores on these tests decide whether or not a company employee will be promoted to a higher position.

Company tests Besides these tests, two important English tests which most Korean college students or company employees take are the TOEFL test and the TOEIC test. The scores on these tests tell how well a person can read, speak, or understand English.

Government tests If a Korean wants to work for the government he or she must take the *kong-mu-won-shi-heom*, or test for government workers. In order to become a diplomat or a representative of the Korean government abroad, a person must take the *ue-mu-go-shi,* or foreign service examination. No matter what Koreans want to do, there is a test that they have to take.

AN ADVERTISEMENT FOR THE TOEIC TEST.

HARD WORDS

- **periodic**: happens from time to time
- **promotion test**: a test to get a better position with a higher pay
- **TOEFL**: Test of English as a Foreign Language, needed to study abroad
- **TOEIC**: Test of English for International Communication, needed to get a job
- **diplomat**: a representative of the government in a Korean embassy or consulate located in a foreign country
- **abroad**: in a foreign country

PRACTICE

MAKE NEW SENTENCES USING THE WORDS IN ORANGE.

...be no end to... 1. trouble...he makes 2. money...she spends 3. things…I lose	THERE SEEMS TO BE NO END TO THE PROBLEMS THAT HE FACES. 
...how well... 4. you...speak English 5. your sister…read 6. he...drive a car	 WHETHER (YOU) GET THE JOB DEPENDS ON HOW WELL YOU CAN USE A COMPUTER.

ANSWERS ON PAGE 122

DISCUSS

1. What do you think about the number of tests that Koreans have to take? Are there too many? Tell why you think so.
   a. It's not a problem. Taking tests is very necessary.
   b. Koreans have to take too many tests. It should be changed.
2. Do you think that people in all other countries have to take the same number of tests that Koreans take, or do Korean take more tests than other people?
3. What do you think is the best way to get a high score on a test? Tell why you think so.
   a. Study each subject a little every day until the day of the test..
   b. Study very hard a few days before the test. That's enough.
4. What do you think of staying up all night (not sleeping) the night before a big test? Have you ever done that? Would you do it again?
5. Korean high school seniors usually sleep very little when they study for the college entrance exam. Is that a good idea not to sleep?
6. How important is English conversation ability on the college entrance exam? Is it important to be able to speak, or is being good at reading and grammar enough?
7. Is cheating on tests a problem in Korean middle schools and high schools? What percentage of the students cheat on tests?
8. Is it possible to get into college by cheating on the college entrance exam?
9. Would you go to a doctor or a dentist who cheated on tests in medical school? Why or why not?

UNIT 5 VIOLENCE NEAR SCHOOLS

TEENAGE GANGS

It's sad that Korean schools are not the safe places that they were just a few years ago. Nowadays some high school students are joining gangs. The gang members beat up or steal money from their classmates and commit other crimes.

Sometimes the victims quit school, move to other school districts, or even commit suicide because they are afraid of the gang members.

Murder In one well-known case of teen gang violence that occurred in 1997, three 15-year-old gang members in Chungnam killed a classmate because he wouldn't obey their orders. They threw him into a lake, knowing that he couldn't swim. The boy drowned, and the three gang members were arrested.

Homepage Gang violence is a big problem in Korea today. Now there is even a homepage on the Internet asking students and parents to report gang violence by email.

GANG VIOLENCE DRIVES SOME STUDENTS TO COMMIT SUICIDE

HARD WORDS

- **beat up**: attack violently
- **victims**: students who are attacked
- **to commit suicide**: kill oneself
- **murder**: to kill, killing someone
- **obey...orders**: do what they told him to do
- **be arrested**: be taken away by the police

JAPANESE COMIC BOOKS ARE ILLEGAL IN KOREA

Korean police are determined to stop these teenage criminals. Besides putting policemen in school areas they're also arresting owners of bars, "phone rooms", and other adults-only entertainment places that admit teenage gang members.

Many Koreans think that Japanese comic books are responsible for the increase of teenage gangs. The comic books teach teenagers how to organize gangs and how to bully weaker students. The comic books have names like "Power Club" and "Speed Gun". The comic books are very popular with Korean teenagers.

The latest trend seems to be teenage "motorcycle gangs" who break traffic laws, fight, snatch purses, and enjoy making a lot of noise.

Why? Why do some teens want to rob or bully their fellow students? It's because of the feeling of power that they get from making other people obey them. They want to feel important. Korean teenagers who join gangs lack parental love and supervision.

A JAPANESE COMIC BOOK ABOUT GANGS AND STREET FIGHTING

HARD WORDS

- **(be) determined**: strongly want to do it, will never stop trying to do it
- **to admit**: allow them to enter
- **to organize**: make a gang, collect gang members
- **to bully**: to attack and hurt other students,
- **snatch purses**: steal women's handbags and then run away quickly
- **lack...supervision**: Their parents don't watch over them and spend time with them.

PRACTICE

MAKE NEW SENTENCES WITH THE WORDS IN ORANGE.

...to obey... 1. Children...parents 2. Dogs...masters 3. Drivers...traffic laws	STUDENTS SHOULD ALWAYS OBEY (THEIR) TEACHERS. 
...to be arrested... 4. He...robbing a store 5. They...stealing a car 6. The boys...fighting	 MY NEIGHBOR WAS ARRESTED FOR DRIVING TOO FAST.

ANSWERS ON PAGE 122

DISCUSS

1. Are there teenage gangs around your school? If so, what do they do? Are they a big problem?
2. Have you ever been afraid to go to school because of teenage gang members who hurt other students? If not, do you have any friends who are afraid of gang members?
3. Have you ever been attacked by gang members? If so, what happened and when did it happen?
4. Why do you think some boys or girls beat up or rob other students? Tell why you think so.
   a. They just want to feel important.
   b. They think it is an easy way to get money.
   c. They're just bad kids who hate school.
5. Who is mostly to blame for the problem of teenage gangs—parents, teachers, or society? Tell why you think so.
6. Why do Japanese comic book makers sell books that make teenagers do bad things? Should they be stopped? Why or why not?
7. What should the police do about the growing teenage motorcycle gang problem in Seoul and other big cities? Can they do anything at all?
8. Can the police do anything to stop teenage gang members from attacking other students? If so, what should they do?
9. Would putting a policeman in every school stop gang members from attacking other students? Would you like to see a policeman in your school? Why or why not?
10. How should gang members who attack other students be punished?

UNIT 6 SEX EDUCATION

TEENAGE PREGNANCY

It is a sad fact that teenage pregnancy is becoming a bigger and bigger problem in Korea. The number of teenagers who are becoming parents is increasing.

TV documentaries have been made about "little moms", the case of a middle school student having a baby was made into a movie. It seems that teenage motherhood has become a trend in Korea. More and more Korean teenagers are becoming sexually active.

Sex education is taught in middle and high schools, but most teachers and experts say that the classes aren't good enough. Instead of fewer girls becoming pregnant each year, more are becoming pregnant.

Unfortunately, the Korean Ministry of Education still doesn't require the teaching of sex education in schools. In 2008 only sixty percent of high school boys in Seoul, Incheon and Kyeonggi-do received some type of sex education, and the average class time was just two and a half hours in a whole year.

SEX EDUCATION IN SCHOOLS IS A BIG ISSUE IN THE USA TOO.

HARD WORDS

- **teenage pregnancy**: girls having babies
- **documentary**: a film to inform, not entertain
- **(be) sexually active**: to be having sex regularly
- **issue**: an important topic now being discussed

The teen years are a difficult time for boys and girls. Their bodies change and they experience romantic love for the first time. They also have strong curiosity about sex. This period is called puberty.

But the traditional Korean thinking about not talking about sex with young people is a problem. It doesn't work in today's world.

The Internet is full of pornography, and Korean chat rooms are being used to find sex partners. More and more teenagers are having sex, and many girls are becoming pregnant. Many teenage boy gangs are committing sex crimes against girls.

Having sex education classes at school could help, but most schools are not teaching the classes. Why not? Maybe because they think that teaching sex education will only make the students want to have sex even more.

But that idea has been proven wrong. Research in the US and other countries shows that students who are given the facts about sex have less sex than students who are not taught anything.

The question is, how long will it take Korea's educational system to catch up to reality? It's becoming a bigger and bigger problem in Korea, and ignoring it isn't going to make it go away.

WRONG! NOT TEACHING SEX EDUCATION CAUSES MORE TEEN PREGNANCY, NOT LESS.

HARD WORDS

- **puberty**: the period when our bodies change from child to adult
- **pornography**: pictures of people having sex
- **to catch...reality**: realize that sex education is needed.
- **to ignore**: not do anything about it; pretend that the problem doesn't exist.

PRACTICE

FILL IN THE CORRECT WORD.

1. Teenage ____is now a problem in Korea.
2. Many more Korean teens are ____active.
3. More and more girls are having ____.
4. Sex education should be given enough ____time.
5. Most teens experience ____love for the first time.
6. ____ is a difficult time for all teenagers.
7. Korea's educational system must catch up to ____.
8. Students who learn sex education have ____ sex.

A. CLASS
B. ROMANTIC
C. SEXUALLY
D. PREGNANCY
E. REALITY
F. BABIES
G. LESS
H. PUBERTY
I. MORE

ANSWERS ON PAGE 122

DISCUSS

1. Does your school teach sex education classes? If so, which students learn the classes—all of the students or just some of the students? Is the class popular with students? Why or why not?
2. Which of these is the biggest sex-related problem in Korea? Tell why.
   a. teenagers having sex
   b. girls having babies
   c. girls having sex for money
   d. bad boys raping (attacking) girls
3. Which of these statements do you agree with and why?
   a. Teaching sex education will just make kids want to have sex.
   b. Teaching sex education will make kids think more carefully about whether or not to have sex.
4. If you think that sex education is a good idea, when (from what age?) is the best time to start teaching it—from elementary school, middle school, high school? Tell why you think so.
5. Did your parents ever teach you anything about sex? Did you ever ask them a question about sex? If your answer to these questions is no, then why didn't you discuss it with your parents?
6. Do you think that teaching sex education will make students have more sex or less sex? Tell why you think so.
7. Do you think that 2½ hours per year is enough time to spend teaching sex education? Can you learn enough in just that much time? How many hours should sex education be taught?
8. What is the main reason why most schools don't teach sex education?
   a. They think it's not necessary.
   b. Teachers won't teach the class.
   c. Schools think teaching sex will make students have more sex.

UNIT 7

PRIVATE INSTITUTES

KOREAN HAGWONS

The Korean government believes that hagwon lessons later than 10 p.m. should be banned. The reason is that the fees charged by cram schools are a huge financial burden on middle class families. If hagwons teach fewer hours, their fees will have to be lower.

Competition Public schools are allowed to have after-school classes until 10 p.m., so banning late night hagwon classes also allows public schools to compete with the hagwons. In 2008 54% of high school students and 80% of middle school students attended hagwons.

Of course hagwon owners and teachers don't agree that the number of study hours should be cut. They don't want to compete with public schools, and they certainly don't want to reduce the amount of money that they take in each month.

But most parents and students like the idea of closing the hagwons earlier. The parents are eager to save money, and students want to go back home earlier.

HARD WORDS

- **(be) banned**: be prohibited, not allowed, against the law
- **cram schools**: a private school for studying to pass the entrance exam.
- **financial burden**: have a lot of money problems
- **to compete**: take some of their students
- **to take in**: to receive (money)

Korean hagwons have been a source of controversy since the 1980s. Back then the government tried to ban them all because only students from rich families could afford to attend. That meant that only rich students could get into the best universities. Poor students didn't stand a chance. Today things are different.

Koreans place a lot of importance on education, and parents are willing to pay a lot of money to send their children to good schools. Hagwons play an important role in the education process in Korea.

Photo: Korea Times

HAGWONS IN SEOUL'S GANGNAM AREA

Not only is it important to go to a hagwon, but it is important to go to the "right" hagwon. Koreans think that whichever hagwon a student attends will make or break his or her chances of getting into a top school.

Of all the hagwons located in Seoul, only 1% of them qualify as preparing students to enter one of the best universities. Some students spend a lot of money traveling a long way to and from home every day to attend these hagwons. The government is hoping to put an end to that.

HARD WORDS

- **source of controversy**: disagreement, different opinions
- **afford**: have enough money to attend
- **stand a chance**: have a chance, be able to attend
- **to make or break**: result in success or failure
- **to qualify**: to be good enough
- **put...to**: stop it, eliminate that expense

PRACTICE

SAY THE SENTENCES REPLACING THE WORDS IN BLUE.

...to stand a chance... 1. He...getting that job 2. She...dating that guy 3. I...getting an A in math.	I DON'T STAND A CHANCE OF GETTING INTO SEOUL UNIVERSITY. 
...to put an end to... 4. I...her phone calls 5. He....his dog's barking 6. She...the baby's crying	 THE POLICE WANT TO PUT AN END TO TEENAGE GANGS.

ANSWERS ON PAGE 122

DISCUSS

1. Do you attend a private institute (hagwon)? If so, how long have you been attending and why do you attend? Are you satisfied with the instruction there? Why or why not?
2. What is your general opinion of private institutes? Tell why you think so.
   a. They are necessary for getting high test scores.
   b. Students don't have to attend private institutes. Regular school classes are enough.
   c. Only English conversation institutes are necessary.
3. Are all private institutes the same, or are some better than others? Tell why you think so.
4. How can you tell (decide) if an institute is good or bad? How important are each of the following?
   a. Instructors (private institute teachers)
   b. Class size (number of students in one class)
   c. Fees (how much money you have to pay to study there)
5. How can you tell if an instructor is good or bad? What is the difference between a good instructor and one who is not so good?
6. Do you agree that hagwon classes should stop at 10 p.m.? Why or why not?
7. Should there be a limit on how much money a hagwon can charge students? Why or why not?
8. Students in English-speaking countries don't have to attend hagwons. Would you like to see the same system in Korea? Why or why not?

UNIT 8

CHOOSING A CAREER

DECIDING ON A MAJOR

High school is a time for making decisions about the future. One of the most important decisions a college-bound student has to make is what to major in. For a few students deciding on a major is easy, but for most students it isn't an easy thing to do.

Some students, such as those interested in mathematics, science or computers may already know that they want to become engineers or doctors even before they get to high school.

But for most other students choosing a college major isn't so simple. The reason is that they are interested in many different things. It is hard for them to decide what kind of a job they want to do for the rest of their lives.

HARD WORDS

- **college-bound student**: a student who plans to attend a college or university (*Don't say, "He goes to university", always "He goes to college." or "He's a college student."*)
- **to major (in)**: to select a certain field of study such as medicine, education, law, etc.
- **a major**: the field of study that you have chosen (*Example: He is majoring in mathematics.*)
- **to get to**: to reach, arrive at

Not too long ago Korean parents usually decided their child's major for them. The deciding factor was how much money they would be able to make. Little or no thought was given to the student's interests or talents. Those things didn't matter.

Since doctors and lawyers made the most money, the law and medical departments of universities were swamped with applications.

Another important factor in deciding a major was the score on the college entrance exam. If the student got a high score, he or she could major in law or medicine, but if the score was lower, he or she would have to plan on a job with a lower salary. Language departments were filled with students who didn't score high enough to get into law or medicine.

Today things are different. Instead of thinking about how much money a future job will bring in, most students are choosing careers that match their interests and abilities. They are majoring in subjects that they like, not subjects that their parents like.

The people who are the most successful in life are people who enjoy their work.

A KID WHO LIKES MATHEMATICS CAN MAJOR IN ECONOMICS OR BECOME A MATH TEACHER

HARD WORDS

- **major**: field of study, such as education, medicine, law, engineering, etc.
- **deciding factor**: the most important thing to be considered
- **talents**: things a person enjoys and can do well
- **(be) swamped (with)**: to have more than can be accepted, (have too much of something)
- **Language departments**: English, German, or Japanese departments

PRACTICE

MAKE NEW SENTENCES USING THE WORDS IN ORANGE.

...to get to... 1. your sister...school 2. his father...work by bus 3. you...Cheju by boat	HOW LONG DID IT TAKE FOR HIM TO GET TO THE HOSPITAL? 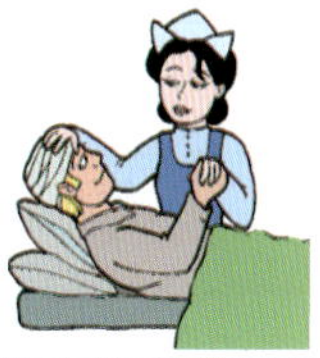
...to be swamped with... 4. My father...office work 5. I...book reports and tests 6. The hospital...new patients	 THE ACTRESS WAS SWAMPED WITH NEW MOVIE OFFERS.

ANSWERS ON PAGE 122

DISCUSS

1. Have you already decided what kind of job or career you want in the future? If so, when did you decide, and why do you want to have that kind of job?
2. Do you already know what you want to major in in college? If not, what are the subjects that you are now thinking of and why?
3. How important was each of the following when deciding upon your future career? Which was the most important and which the least?
   a. Money (how much money you can make in the future)
   b. Your parents (what they want you to study)
   c. Your teachers (what your teachers suggested that you study)
   d. Difficulty (if it's "hard" or "easy")
   e. Your interests (the things that you are interested in the most)
4. Is the career that you chose similar to the career of one of your parents or is it completely different? Would there be any advantage in doing a job that one of your parents does? If so, what?
5. Which career fields will be the most important in Korea during this century? Which will earn the most money? Tell why you think so.
   a. English education (teaching)
   b. Farming
   c. Computer science
   d. International business
   e. Travel industry
   f. Hotel industry
   g. Discount store retailing
   h. Space exploration
   i. Government work
   j. Health care (doctors, nurses)
6. How important will English ability be in the job career that you have chosen—very important, a little important, or not at all?

UNIT 9

GOING TO COLLEGE

THE COLLEGE YEARS

Attending a university in Korea isn't the same as going to a university in the USA. It's easy to get into college in the U.S. but in Korea it's very hard.

No entrance exam There is no national college entrance exam in the U.S. Each school chooses its students independently. In Korea there are too many students who want to go to college and not enough colleges, so the competition to get in is fierce. The exam is very hard, and some students cannot pass.

It's hard to get into a Korean university, but it's easy to graduate. In the USA it's easy to get into college but very hard to graduate. Many students who start college in the USA do not graduate. They flunk out.

COLLEGE CLASSES ARE MUCH DIFFERENT FROM HIGH SCHOOL CLASSES.

HARD WORDS

- **college**: The word *university* is used only when saying the name of the school.
- **independently**: doing it by themselves
- **competition...fierce**: many students trying to enter the same universities
- **to flunk out**: fail, have to quit school because of bad grades

One thing that is the same about going to college in Korea and in the US is that it can be the most exciting time in a person's life. Besides learning many things and preparing themselves for future careers, college students can form some of the best friendships they will have during their lives.

School clubs There are many extracurricular activities in colleges—everything from music clubs to hiking clubs to English and science clubs. Whatever a student's interests happen to be, he or she can find a school club to join.

But college life is more than just joining clubs and making friends. In today's tough job market students have to study harder to make employers want to hire them. No employer wants to hire a person who made bad grades in college.

Study or play? College students are freer than high school students to make their own decisions. They can decide when to study and when to have fun. Many students make the wrong decisions, party too much, then have to drop out of school.

COLLEGE STUDENT DRINKING BEER FROM A HOSE

HARD WORDS

- **extracurricular activities:** school clubs and sports
- **tough job market**: very hard to find a job
- **to party** (verb): to play and have a good time
- **hose**: like the one used to carry water

BOY WITH A HOSE

PRACTICE

SAY THE SENTENCES USING THE WORDS IN ORANGE.

...to get into... 1. He tried...school...but failed 2. I wanted...the club...gave up 3. I tried...meeting...couldn't.	THE COMPETITION TO GET INTO COLLEGE IS VERY FIERCE. 
...to decide whether 4. You...stay here or go home 5. They...do homework or play 6. He...play tennis or soccer	 STUDENTS CAN DECIDE WHETHER TO STUDY OR PLAY.

ANSWERS ON PAGE 122

DISCUSS

1. Are you planning to go to college? If so, what kind of college or university do you want to attend? Why?
2. Does it matter very much which college or university a student attends? Tell why you think so.
3. Why are some colleges or universities ranked higher than others? What makes one school better than another? What are the things that make a college great?
4. Do you think that every high school student should go to college, or should some students not go to college? Why do you think so?
5. If you could not pass the college entrance exam the first time, what would you do—take the test again, study abroad, or give up? Why?
6. Many college students in the U.S. have part-time jobs to earn money and pay for their tuition. Should Korean students do that too? Why or why not?
7. More college students flunk out of school in the USA than in Korea. Does that mean that Koreans study harder or that American schools are harder? Tell why you think so.
8. Is there any advantage to attending a foreign university? If so, what?
9. What percentage of a college student's time should be spent on sports and going to parties? Tell why you think so.
   a. 10% or less. College is for studying, not for having a good time.
   b. 30%. Study is more important, but students need to have fun too.
   c. 80%. The main reason for going to college is to have fun.

UNIT 10 STUDYING ABROAD

KOREAN STUDENTS OVERSEAS

The idea of attending college in a foreign country instead of in Korea began to catch on in the mid-1990s. In 1996 Korean newspapers reported that more than 2,000 Korean students were studying abroad. But by 2008 that number had grown to an amazing 216,827 students, 70% of them in the United States. In 2009 a weaker Korean won forced many of those students to return home.

But if given a choice between studying in Korea or studying abroad, most Korean students will choose to go abroad.

There are two reasons why many Korean students want to study abroad:

- **It is easier to get into a foreign university than a Korean university.** Each year half of the students who want to enroll in Korean universities fail the entrance test. Instead of trying again, many of them just get a passport and enroll in a foreign college or university.

YOU NEED A PASSPORT TO GO TO A FOREIGN COUNTRY.

HARD WORDS

- **overseas**: abroad, in foreign countries
- **to catch on**: become popular
- **a...won**: cheap compared to the US dollar and the money of other countries (need more won to pay for things)
- **to enroll**: to register as a student

English is the key to success. In today's connected world, people who know English get the best jobs. Speaking only Korean isn't enough anymore.

But studying abroad isn't for everyone. It is very expensive, so only people who have enough money can do it. Besides that, a good score on the TOEFL test is necessary before you can apply.

For a student who has never traveled outside of Korea, adjusting to life in a foreign country can be hard. Customs are different, and getting used to the food can be a problem.

Making friends might be hard, especially at the beginning, and without close friends, life in a faraway place can be very lonely. Some students get homesick and return home.

New Freedom But many students who make the adjustment to foreign life say that life abroad is better than life in Korea in some ways. They can speak their minds more freely than in Korea. They can also wear whatever kind of clothes they want without caring what other people will think.

Asians worry a lot about saving face, but people in western countries don't care very much about that. Living in a foreign culture that is more liberal than Korea makes many students not want to return home.

FIRST YOU HAVE TO GET A GOOD SCORE ON THE TOEFL TEST

HARD WORDS

- **connected world**: instant communication among countries
- **(be) homesick**: be lonely and want to go back home
- **speak...minds**: say whatever they want to say
- **to save face**: not do or say things that make other people not like you
- **liberal**: open-minded, do whatever you want, anything is okay

PRACTICE

SAY THE SENTENCES USING THE WORDS IN ORANGE.

...to catch on 1. Long hair…mid-1960s 2. The internet...1990s 3. Studying abroad...1996	HIP HOP MUSIC CAUGHT ON IN THE 1980S. 
...to get used to... 4. He...eating Indian food. 5. They...traveling by plane. 6. I...Seoul's cold winters	 I COULD NEVER GET USED TO LIVING ON A FARM.

ANSWERS ON PAGE 122

DISCUSS

1. Do you know anyone who went abroad to study? If so, who was it, and why did they decide to go?
2. Where would you rather attend college—in Korea or at a foreign university? Tell why.
3. Which of the following do you think would be your biggest problem if you went abroad to study? Tell why you think so.
   a. Making friends
   b. Homesickness (missing my family and friends in Korea)
   c. Getting used to the food
   d. Having to speak English all the time
4. What would be the most exciting thing about studying in a foreign country? Tell why you think so.
   a. Meeting people who can't speak Korean
   b. Speaking English all the time
   c. Traveling and seeing new places
   d. Learning about new customs and way of thinking
5. Could it be easier to live in a foreign country than in Korea? Discuss:
   a. Speaking one's mind—being free to say whatever you want
   b. Saving face—not having to worry about what other people think
6. What is the main reason why Korean students want to study abroad? Tell why you think so.
7. When is the best time to study abroad—elementary school, middle or high school, or college? Tell why you think so.
8. If you could study abroad, where would you go and why?

UNIT 11 THE PAINS OF GROWING UP

THE TEENAGE YEARS

It isn't easy to be a teenager. The teenage years are filled with problems of all kinds. A teenager is no longer a child but not yet an adult. Teenagers are searching for a sense of identity. This difficult time of life is called *adolescence*.

Physical changes The name for the period when a teenager's body develops sexually is puberty. It begins around age 11 for girls and age 13 for boys. During puberty boys change into young men and girls become young women. By the time they are 14 or 15 their bodies are sexually mature. That means they are able to have children of their own.

Adolescence can be a time of stress because all teenagers don't develop at the same speed. Some teens worry that they're not growing as fast as their friends are. Teens who are smaller than their friends are afraid that they might never grow up.

Other teenagers worry that they're too tall, too fat, too thin, or too ugly. Every teenager worries about something.

HARD WORDS

- **teenager**: between 13- and 19-years old
- **a...identity**: deciding who they are
- **puberty**: going from child to adult
- **to grow up**: to become an adult

Teenagers are very concerned about their appearance. Clothes and hair styles are very important to them. They usually feel that they have to wear the same kind of clothes and hair styles that their friends are wearing.

Peer pressure Teenagers also have a strong desire to be liked by their peers. Sometimes they do things just to please or impress their friends. What makes them do those things is called *peer pressure*. Sometimes pleasing friends involves taking chances.

Teenagers want to try out new things. They also crave excitement. That's why many teenagers try drinking or smoking cigarettes or do other things that are bad for them.

A sense of identity Besides growing taller and maturing sexually, teenagers start to think and feel differently. They start to make close friendships outside the family. They start to get ideas of their own. Teenagers spend a lot of time talking on the phone with friends.

Sometimes their new behavior causes arguments with family members, but that is normal for teenagers. It is a teenager's way of becoming an individual.

TEENAGERS SEARCH FOR A SENSE OF IDENTITY

HARD WORDS

- **peers**: other people who are the same age
- **impress**: make other people admire them
- **taking chances**: doing dangerous things
- **crave excitement**: want to do exciting things
- **get...own**: start to think differently from their parents
- **become...individual**: make their own decisions

BREAKING AWAY

PRACTICE

SAY THE SENTENCES USING THE WORDS IN PINK.

...ideas of (his) own 1. She.... 2. They... 3. My brother...	HE'S JUST 5 YEARS OLD, BUT ALREADY HE HAS IDEAS OF HIS OWN. 
...to impress 4. My boyfriend...teachers 5. You...teachers 6. Our friends...teachers	 SHE TRIES HARD TO IMPRESS HER STUDENTS.

ANSWERS ON PAGE 122

DISCUSS

1. Do you think it's hard to be a teenager? If so, why is it hard?
2. How important are each of the following things to you? Tell why.
   a. ...wearing popular clothes and hairstyles
   b. ...being able to make my own decisions
   c. ...being liked by other students and my friends
3. Do you carry a cellular phone? If so, why do you have it?
   a. I thought it would be fun and I need one. Why?
   b. I wanted to feel grown up (be like an adult)
   c. All of my friends have them. (peer pressure)

4. Have you ever done anything with friends that was "bad" for you? If so, what was it, and why did you do it?
5. Do you sometimes have arguments with your parents? If so, what do you argue about?
   a. My clothes
   b. My friends
   c. My behavior
   d. My hair
   e. School
   f. going to college
6. Do you always do what your parents tell you to do? Why or why not?
7. Have you ever made a decision that you later regretted? If so, did you learn anything from that experience? Would you do it again?
8. When do you think is (will be) the best (most enjoyable) time of your life—childhood, high school, college? Why do you think so?
9. Do you sometimes worry about things? What kinds of things do you worry about the most?
   a. My appearance / clothes
   b. School work / college exam
   c. My social life
   d. ____?______

UNIT 12 FAMILY RELATIONSHIPS

BREAKING AWAY

The outside world But when children turn into teenagers they have to form their own lives outside the family and learn about the outside world. And so they start to make close personal relationships outside the home.

When this happens parents often feel rejected. They see their children becoming more and more independent. They realize that their children are breaking away from the family.

Until the age of 12 or 13 the center of a child's life is the family. His parents take care of him in every way and make all of his decisions for him. All important activities are done with the family. A child's home is the center of his or her world.

A YOUNG CHILD'S FAMILY IS THE CENTER OF ITS LIFE

HARD WORDS

- **turn into**: become
- **close...relationships**: good friends
- **feel rejected**: feel not liked or wanted
- **break away**: make a life outside home

TEENAGERS FIND MANY FUN THINGS TO DO AWAY FROM HOME

Life in Korea today is much different from the past. The home isn't the center of entertainment for everyone in the family anymore. Today there are many interesting things to do and many exciting places to go outside the home.

An Independent Lifestyle Most Korean families have cars, often two cars. Mothers and fathers both have busy schedules with things to do and places to go. So today's teenagers have more opportunities than ever before to become independent.

But teenagers have to remember that having an exciting private life outside the home doesn't mean that family relationships aren't important.

Pressures Teenagers have a lot of problems to solve. Sometimes the pressures of life are so bad that they may want to run away from everyone and everything. But asking a parent or an older brother or sister for advice is sometimes just what it takes to solve a difficult problem. Teens who have close relationships with family members are the lucky ones because when they need advice they don't have far to go.

TEENAGERS SOMETIMES NEED HELP FROM PARENTS

HARD WORDS

- **center of entertainment**: the place where you have the most fun
- **private life**: having close friendships and doing things with friends
- **pressures of life**: the many problems that a teenager faces
- **just what it takes**: the perfect way to solve the problem

PRACTICE

FILL IN THE CORRECT WORD.

1. The family is the _____ of a young child's world.
2. Every child_____ a teenager.
3. Teenagers make close_____ outside the home.
4. Sometimes parents feel_____ by their sons or daughters.
5. Teenagers start to_____ away from home.
6. Many parents have very busy_____.
7. Today's Koreans have an_____ lifestyle.
8. Today's teenagers have many_____ of life.

A. CENTER
B. REJECTED
C. SCHEDULES
D. TURNS INTO
E. PRESSURES
F. INDEPENDENT
G. ADVICE
H. RELATIONSHIPS
I. BREAK

ANSWERS ON PAGE 123

DISCUSS

1. How many are there in your family (includes parents, brothers and sisters)? Do you have a close relationship with any of them?
2. If you have any brothers and sisters, what was your position in the birth order—oldest, second, youngest, etc.? If you were not first born, would you like to be? Why or why not?
3. When you have an important personal problem, who do you ask for advice? Why?
   a. a parent
   b. a brother or sister
   c. a close friend or classmate
   d. a teacher
   e. no one, I solve the problem by myself
4. Which of these subjects would you talk to your parents about? Which would you *never* discuss with your parents? Why not?
   a. friends
   b. school and homework
   c. money
   d. a boyfriend or girlfriend
   e. sex or love
   f. smoking
   g. cheating on tests

5. If you become a parent in the future and have children of your own, are there any kinds of problems that you would NOT talk about with your children? What kind of problems, and why not?
6. Do you feel that you've broken away from your family? If so, when did it first start to happen—at what age?
7. Where do you have the most fun in your life—at home or with friends outside the home? What are your favorite things to do?
8. At what age (how old?) should a person get his or her first cell phone? Tell why you think so.

UNIT 13 CHOOSING FRIENDS

MAKING CHOICES

The friends that a person chooses in high school can make a lot of difference in his or her future. Teenagers are easily influenced by the people around them, so the kind of person they turn out to be depends on the kind of friends that they have. For this reason teenagers need to choose their friends wisely.

If you make friends with other students who are honest, study hard, and plan to go to college, you'll probably study hard and make plans for college too.

But if you hang out with friends who smoke, drink, and hate school, you'll probably be the same kind of person. Your school grades will be bad, and you probably won't be learning English.

DO THESE BOYS HAVE GOOD OR BAD GRADES AT SCHOOL?

HARD WORDS

- **(be) influenced by**: do the same things, learn from them
- **turn...be**: become
- **to make friends (with)**: become friends with
- **to hang out (with)**: spend your free time with, go places with
- **grades**: marks, test scores (A, B-, C+...)

Best Friends Every high school student needs to have someone he or she considers to be a "best friend"—someone to tell troubles to, someone to have fun with outside of school.

It's especially important to have someone like that when you are growing up. Teenagers face many problems so they need to have someone who can give them comfort and support when their problems seem to be too much to bear.

Best friends are often inseparable. They go to school together, and they go shopping together. They spend a lot of time talking on the phone.

A person's best friend might be an older brother or sister, but for most teenagers it's a classmate. That's because a classmate can usually relate to their daily lives better than an older brother or sister can.

TEENAGERS SHARE SECRETS WITH THEIR BEST FRIENDS

HARD WORDS

- **to tell...to**: to discuss one's problems with, to get advice about
- **give...support**: give advice, make them feel better
- **too...bear**: can't endure
- **(be) inseparable**: be together almost all the time
- **to relate (to)**: can imagine themselves in the same situation

PRACTICE

MAKE NEW SENTENCES USING THE WORDS IN PINK.

...to hang out 1. She.... 2. They... 3. My brother...	I HANG OUT WITH THE SAME FRIENDS THAT I GREW UP WITH. 
...to relate to 4. He... son 5. She...kids 6. They...daughter	 PARENTS CAN'T RELATE TO THE LIVES OF THEIR TEENAGE CHILDREN.

ANSWERS ON PAGE 123

DISCUSS

1. Is there one person who is your best friend? If so, when did you meet and how (why) did you become best friends?
2. Is it important for a person to have a best friend? Why or why not?
3. Is it better to have a few close friends and no best friend? Tell why you think so.
4. How many close friends do you have? What kind of things do you do when you're together?
5. Do you and your best friend tell secrets to each other? If so, what kind of secrets do you tell each other (about what things)?
6. It is said that you can know a lot about a person just by looking at his or her friends. Do you agree? Why or why not?
7. When do people form their strongest friendships in life—elementary school, middle or high school, college, when they start working? Tell why you think so.
8. Is it possible for two brothers or sisters to be best friends, or do best friends always have to be people from outside the family? Tell why you think so.
9. What do you do when you or your best friend wants to do something that the other one doesn't want to do?
   a. We don't do it.
   b. We do something else.
   c. We separate (one does it while the other one doesn't.)
10. Do your parents ever talk to you about your friends, or do they not care about what kind of friends you have?
11. If your parents didn't like one of your friends would you stop hanging out with that person? Why or why not?

UNIT 14

THE OPPOSITE SEX

TEENAGE CRUSHES

Most people experience the first feeling of romantic love when they are teenagers. They see or meet someone who attracts them and instantly, they are "in love". At least, they *think* it is love that they feel. If the person is a teenager we usually call the feeling a *teenage crush.* High school girls often have crushes on their young male teachers. Teenage crushes usually don't last long—only until they see someone else who looks even better.

A Controversial subject Since teenagers are developing emotionally, it is natural for them to have crushes. When two people like each other they usually want to be together. And so they decide to date.

The subject of high school dating is still controversial in Korea. Most high school kids think it's okay, but most parents and teachers disagree.

NOT EVERYBODY AGREES THAT DATING IN HIGH SCHOOL IS OKAY

HARD WORDS

- **romantic love**: falling in love
- **to last**: to continue
- **to develop emotionally**: learn about love and romance
- **to date** (verb): to go on dates together
- **controversial**: something that people disagree over, have different opinions about

Since Korean teenagers study in all-boy or all-girl classes, they are very curious about the opposite sex. They can only meet with members of the opposite sex outside of class. The only way they can spend time together is by dating.

To study or to date? Some parents don't mind if their teenage sons and daughters date, but they are the exceptions. Most Korean parents and teachers think that high school students need to spend their time studying, especially if they want to go to a good university. They think that students who go out on dates won't be able to get high scores on the college entrance exam.

For students who date, popular places to go on dates are public parks, movie theaters, or fast food restaurants. Most teenagers who date don't much care where they go, as long as they can be together.

STUDENTS AT ALL-GIRLS SCHOOLS HAVE FEWER CHANCES TO MEET BOYS

HARD WORDS

- **(be) curious**: they want to know about...
- **the opposite sex:**: There are two sexes—males and females.
- **to spend**: Same as *use*
- **exceptions**: people who think differently from the others
- **don't...care**: It doesn't matter to them

PRACTICE

SAY THE SENTENCES USING THE WORDS IN PINK.

...to last 1. The birthday party...2 hours 2. The rain...just 10 minutes 3. A cell phone...a few years	THE MOVIE LASTED A LONG TIME. 
...to spend 4. She…10,000 won a week 5. I...5000 won yesterday 6. We...5 hours studying last night	 STUDENTS SPEND A LONG TIME AT SCHOOL EVERY DAY.

ANSWERS ON PAGE 123

DISCUSS

1. How much time do you spend thinking about the opposite sex—a lot of time, just a little time, or no time at all?
2. What do you think about having members of the opposite sex in the same school? Tell why you think so.
    a. It makes learning more fun.
    b. It's a distraction. I like same-sex schools better.
3. Have you ever had a "crush" on a girl or a boy? If so, how old were you? How long did the crush last? How did you feel at the time?
4. Why do you think that many high school students get crushes on their young teachers? Have you ever had a crush like that? If so, which teacher?
5. When do you think is the best time for people to start dating? Why do you think so?
    a. in middle school
    b. in high school
    c. in college

6. How do your parents feel about you going out on dates?
7. If a boy and a girl go out on a date, who should pay—the boy, the girl, or 50/50 (Dutch treat)?
8. Is it okay for girls to date boys who are older than they are? How about dating boys younger than they are?
9. Which is more fun—hanging out with your close friends or going out on a date?
10. Some students prefer to be with same sex friends than with members of the opposite sex. Do you think they're strange, or is that okay?

UNIT 15 MODERN KOREA

LIFESTYLE CHANGES

Korea has changed a lot in the past few decades. In many ways Korea isn't the same place that it was 25 or 30 years ago. It's like a different country.

Fast Food Today Koreans love to eat hamburgers and pizzas, but before the 1988 Olympics there were no hamburger or pizza fast food restaurants in the country. In fact, there were no fast food restaurants at all!

Today Korea's expressways are jammed with cars, but 25 years ago almost all cars on the roads were taxis. Today most people over 18 have driver's licenses, but in 1985 only a few Koreans had licenses, and almost all of them were men!

New Shopping Habits. Koreans now shop differently from the way they used to shop. 25 years ago most shopping took place at shijangs, where you could buy everything from food to clothes to electrical appliances. Prices were not marked, so customers haggled with shop owners for lower prices.

Today Koreans prefer to shop at big discount stores like E-Mart or Lotte Mart, where they can buy everything and prices are already low.

DISCOUNT STORES ARE VERY POPULAR IN KOREA

HARD WORDS

- **(be) jammed (with)**: be crowded with (cars, trucks, and buses)
- **shijang**: also called "flea market" or "outdoor market"
- **electrical appliances**: refrigerator, washing machine, toaster, etc.
- **to haggle**: to argue for a lower price

There are a few reasons why Koreans are abandoning the open markets.

1. For one thing, most people now drive cars, so they need places to park. Shijangs don't have parking lots, but discount stores do.

2. Because discount stores have indoor parking lots, it's convenient to go shopping even when it's raining or cold outside. The stores are warm in winter and cool in summer. Shijangs are cold in winter and hot in summer.

A TRADITIONAL OPEN MARKET

3. Discount stores have huge selections, prices are low, and customers don't have to haggle over prices. Most discount stores are open 24 hours a day, but shijangs close at night.

Years ago only women went shopping for food, but today we can see many men pushing shopping carts. It has become acceptable for men to go shopping at supermarkets.

In the 1980s, most Korean men wouldn't want to be seen shopping in a supermarket because shopping was supposed to be "woman's work".

KOREAN MEN USED TO BE ASHAMED TO BE SEEN PUSHING A SHOPPING CART

HARD WORDS

- **to abandon**: give up, stop doing it
- **huge selections**: a lot of products to choose from
- **Years ago...**: many years ago, a long time ago
- **has...acceptable**: it's okay if they do it
- **want...seen**: would feel embarrassed if other people saw them

PRACTICE

SAY THE SENTENCES ADDING SOME MISSING WORDS.

...be jammed with 1. Stores..?.. on Sunday 2. Subways…people…? 3. The beach…?...summer	KOREAN ROADS **ARE JAMMED WITH** CARS EVERY DAY. 
...to be seen... 4. men...in a dress shop 5. women…without makeup 6. teachers...at a nightclub	 MOST BOYS WOULDN'T WANT TO **BE SEEN** IN THEIR UNDERWEAR.

DISCUSS

ANSWERS ON PAGE 123

1. Can you remember what Korea was like when you were a little child? Has anything changed since then? If so, what?
2. Do you sometimes go to fast food restaurants? Would you be happy if there were no fast food restaurants in Korea, like in the 1980s? Why or why not?
3. Where do you prefer to shop—at the shijang or at a discount store? Why do you like to shop there? Where does your mother shop?
4. These are some things that you have today but most people didn't have or didn't even exist in Korea 25 years ago. Could you be happy if you didn't have them? Why or why not?
   a. cell phones
   b. computers
   c. the Internet
   d. digital cameras

   e. DVD players
   f. discount stores
   g. private cars
   h. cable television

5. What do you think about Korean men being ashamed to be seen shopping in a supermarket during the 1980s? Tell why you think so.
   a. I think they were right. Supermarkets are only for women.
   b. That is ridiculous. Supermarkets are for everybody.
6. Why do you think that only men were drivers in the 1980s? How has Korean thinking changed since then?
7. What is the future of the Korean shijang? Will Korea always have open markets or will the markets someday be replaced by discount stores? Tell why you think so.
8. Nothing has changed life in Korea as much as the private car, which almost nobody had in the 1980s. How has private car ownership made life different from 20 or 30 years ago?

CITY LIFE, COUNTRY LIFE

FROM FARM TO CITY

Korea recently made the transition from a developing country to an advanced country. Advanced countries are industrialized, but developing countries are mostly agricultural. Thirty years ago most Koreans were farmers, but today more Koreans work in factories or office buildings than on farms.

Back then, Korea's economy was driven by exporting agricultural products, but today the products being exported are made in factories.

Rapid development. Korea's development happened quickly. It was only about 30 years ago when the movement from the farms to the cities began. Life on a farm is hard, so it is not surprising that many young people from farming areas wanted to move to the cities. There they could get jobs in factories or with big companies.

In 1980 about 20% of Koreans lived on farms, but by 1995 the number of Koreans living in rural areas had been cut in half.

HARD WORDS

- **(be) industrialized**: most people work for factories or big companies
- **(be) agricultural**: be mostly farmers
- **driven...products**: they sold farm products such as rice to other countries
- **Rapid development**: got rich quickly
- **rural areas**: farming communities in the countryside

There are several reasons why young people wanted to leave the farms and go to the city. The most important reason was to make more money. Everyone knows that farmers work hard but don't make much money. A factory worker can make much more money while working fewer hours.

More Free Time Another reason to move was to have more free time. Farmers don't have much time to relax, but people who work in the cities do. They can also have a social life. There are lots of fun things to do in the city.

Most people who live on farms go to bed early and get up early, but people who live in the cities go to bed later and get up later.

But cities are also noisy and have traffic jams. Also, the air is dirty because of all of the cars, trucks and buses.

Farming communities are quiet and have clean air. For that reason, some people who move to the cities later wish that they still lived in the country.

HARD WORDS

- **to have...life**: have friends and go places with them
- **fun things**: activities that are a lot of fun
- **in the country**: in the countryside, farming areas

PRACTICE

MAKE NEW SENTENCES USING THE WORDS IN ORANGE.

...to be cut in half 1. The amount of homework… 2. College tuition… 3. The number of students...	THE PRICE OF FLAT-SCREEN TVS HAS BEEN CUT IN HALF. 
...to wish... 4. She...had a lot of money 5. He...could buy a new car 6. They...could move to Cheju	 SOME PEOPLE WISH THEY STILL LIVED IN THE COUNTRY.

ANSWERS ON PAGE 123

DISCUSS

1. Which of these places do you think is the best place to live? Tell why you think so.

   a. a very big city
   b. a suburb (area near a big city)
   c. a small city or town near the countryside
   d. a rural (farming) area

2. What are some things you can do in cities but you can't do in the country?
3. What are some advantages of living in the country instead of living in a big city?
4. Where is the best place for people to live when they get old and stop working? Tell why you think so.
5. Where would you rather live--a big house in the country or a small apartment in a high apartment building near a big city? Tell why you think so.
6. Where is the best place to do each of the following—city or country? Tell why.
   a. Go shopping
   b. Go jogging or ride a bicycle
   c. Go to high school
   d. Go to the movies
   e. Spend time with friends
   f. Go swimming
   g. Learn English
   h. Learn to drive a car
7. Will many people who now live in cities start moving back to the countryside someday? If not, why won't that happen? Why will city living always be more popular than country living?

SAFETY AWARENESS

CHILD SAFETY SEATS

Child safety seats are the equivalent of seat belts for children. If adults are forced to use safety belts when riding in a car, why not children too?

Actually, the use of car seats for babies and small children has been a law in Korea since 1990, but most Korean parents do not obey the law.

No. 1 cause of death. Korean parents are the number one cause of the death of children in car crashes. That's because they don't put their children into child safety seats.

The seats prevent death in 70% of car crashes, and they prevent serious injury 67% of the time. So most of the children who are killed or injured in car crashes every year would have just minor injuries if their parents used the safety seats.

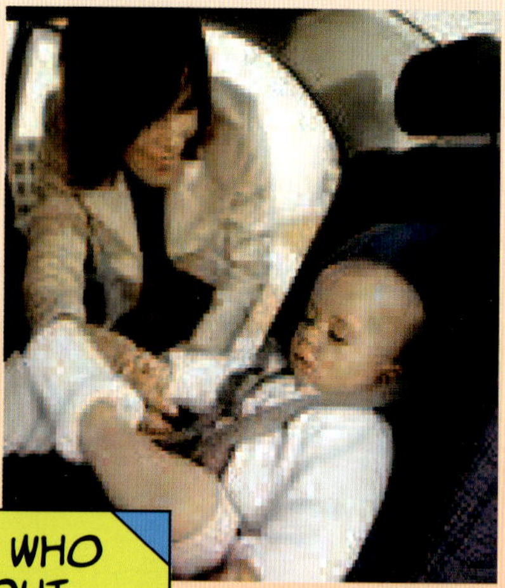

A MOTHER WHO THINKS ABOUT CHILD SAFETY

HARD WORDS

- **(be) the...of:** is the same as
- **(be) forced to:** the law makes them do it
- **to obey:** to do it, do what the law says that you must do
- **prevent death:** make people not die
- **serious / minor injury:** hurt badly / hurt just a little

Some people might ask, why can't children use the same safety belts that adults use? Why do parents have to buy a special child's seat that costs a lot of money?

It is because children are too small for regular safety belts. In an accident, the belts could actually kill them instead of saving them.

BOOSTER SEAT FOR OLDER CHILDREN

A REGULAR SEAT BELT CAN KILL A BABY IN AN ACCIDENT

Booster seats Children more than 4 years old are too big for child safety seats, but they are still too small for regular seat belts. These children need something called a *booster seat*. A booster seat can be used with a regular seat belt because the child sits higher.

The main reasons why most parents don't obey the law are: a) the children complain, b) parents don't want to spend the money to buy the seats, c) parents think it's too much trouble and d) the police don't enforce the law.

A POLICEMAN ENFORCING THE LAW

HARD WORDS

- **to save them**: to allow them to live, not die
- **to complain:** cry, make noise because they don't like it
- **(be) too...trouble:** They don't want to take the time to do it
- **to enforce**: make the people do it

PRACTICE

MAKE NEW SENTENCES BY ADDING SOME WORDS .

1. Child safety seats are the _____of seat belts.
2. Adults are _____to use seat belts when riding in a car.
3. Safety belts can prevent serious _____in a crash.
4. Korean parents should _____the law.
5. Parents should always think about child _____.
6. Older children should use a _____ seat.
7. Children sometimes _____ about using a safety seat.
8. Parents may think it's too much _____ to use the seats.

A. INJURY
B. OBEY
C. EQUIVALENT
D. COMPLAIN
E. BOOSTER
D. TROUBLE
G. FORCED
H. SAFETY

ANSWERS ON PAGE 123

DISCUSS

1. Before studying this unit, what did you think of child safety seats?
   a. I thought they were a good idea.
   b. I thought they were unnecessary.
   c. I never heard of child safety seats.
2. After reading about child safety seats, what do you think now? Tell why you think so.
   a. I think all small children should be put into safety seats.
   b. I still think they are not necessary.
3. Do you always wear a seat belt in a car? Why or why not?
4. If people have to use seat belts, shouldn't children have to use them too? Why or why not?
5. Do most Korean people think more about safety or speed (doing something fast)? How about you?
6. Since Korean police enforce the seat belt law, why don't they enforce the law about child safety seats?
7. When riding in a car, where is the best place for a baby to be? Tell why you think so.
   a. The baby should be in a child safety seat.
   b. The mother should hold the baby in the back seat.
8. Does your school teach students about safety? What rules of safety, if any, does your school have in place?
9. Korea has one of the highest traffic accidents records in the world. Why do you think there are so many traffic accidents in Korea?
10. What does Korea have to do to improve its safety record? Tell why you think so.

UNIT 18

REUNIFICATION

BIG PROBLEMS

Most South Koreans dream of reunification with the North. But is it really possible? It won't be easy. The two countries have two very different kinds of governments, and each of them hates the other kind.

A democracy vs. a dictatorship

South Korea is a democracy. It has a president who is chosen by the citizens. North Korea is a police state with a dictator who is not chosen by the people but who makes all of the laws by himself.

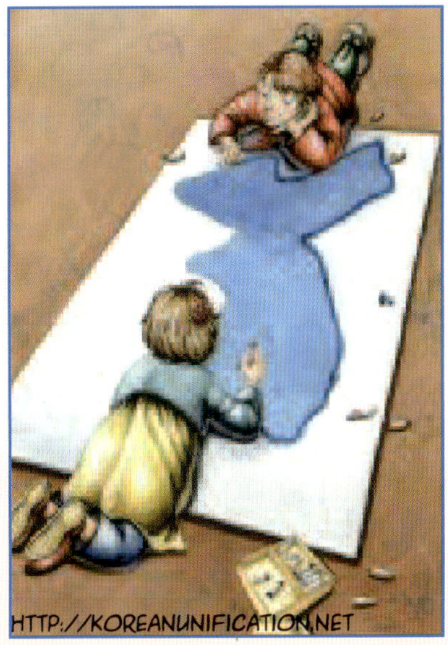

People in a democracy are free to move, travel to foreign countries, and buy whatever they want. They can even criticize their leaders.

North Koreans can't do any of those things. They aren't allowed to travel even inside their own country, and all of their news is censored.

If they say anything bad about their leaders, they are either killed or sent to prison.

2 DIFFERENT WORLDS

HARD WORDS

- **reunification**: become one country again.
- **police state**: the people are like prisoners
- **dictator**: one man who decides everything
- **to criticize**: to say bad things against
- **be censored**: only some of the news is reported, the other part is hidden

SOUTHERNERS CAN BUY WHAT-EVER THEY WANT

Korea was divided into two parts long ago, and now the two countries don't have much in common except their history and their language. Also their ways of thinking and their lifestyles are totally different.

Now some South Koreans are not eager for reunification because the North is too undeveloped and poor. Reunification will be very expensive, and the South will have to pay for everything.

South Korea is a modern industrialized country. It is one of the richest countries in Asia. South Koreans use computers, drive new cars, wear expensive clothes and live in nice apartments and houses.

North Koreans are poor, don't have enough food to eat and live in homes without lights, telephones or appliances. Foreigners who have visited North Korea say that the country has not changed at all since the 1950s.

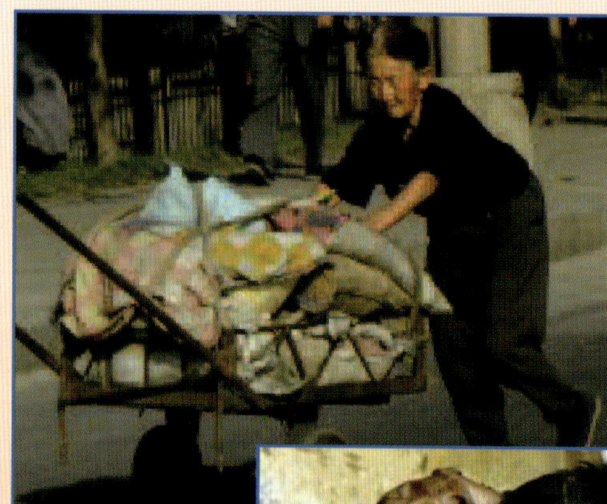

NORTH KOREANS CAN'T BUY ANYTHING

HARD WORDS

- **industrialized**: have a lot of factories and businesses
- **appliances**: things like refrigerators and washing machines
- **have...common**: be the same in many ways
- **undeveloped**: still live like long ago, nothing modern

PRACTICE

FILL IN THE CORRECT WORD

1. You can buy___ you want.
2. You can go___ you want.
3. You can visit___ you want.
4. They don't have enough___ to eat.
5. She doesn't have enough___ to drink.
6. I don't have enough___ to spend.

A. FOOD
B. WHATEVER
C. MILK
D. WHOEVER
E. CLOTHES
F. WHENEVER
G. MONEY

ANSWERS ON PAGE 123

DISCUSS

1. Do you agree with A or B? Tell why you agree.
   a. The North and the South should reunify because the countries share the same history and the same language.
   b. The North and the South cannot reunify because their ways of thinking are too different.
2. Why will the South have to pay all of the cost of reunification? Why doesn't the North have to pay for anything?
3. After reunification, should all North and South Koreans live together, or should North Koreans live separately? Tell why you think so.

4. If the people from the north all live separately from southerners, how will Korean society be changed?
5. After reunification, will some people from the south go to live in the north, or will people just come from north to south? Which southerners will go north? To do what?
6. Why does reunification cost a lot of money? What things will the money be spent on?
7. After reunification comes, will more Korean people still live in the south, or will people spread out evenly all over the country from north to south? Tell why you think so.
8. If the border between north and south were opened tomorrow, what percent of the North Korean people would come to the south immediately? Tell why you think so.
9. Would any South Koreans move to the North? Why or why not?
10. If you see a person on the street, can you tell if it's a South Korean or a North Korean? Do they look different or the same?
11. Do both countries have the same customs or are they different?

UNIT 19 TEENAGE DEFECTORS

FROM THIS...

...TO THIS

FITTING IN

More than 10,000 North Korean defectors now live in South Korea. All of them came because they were hungry for food and freedom. For most North Koreans life is a nightmare of poverty and death. They are like prisoners in their own country.

Many of the defectors were teenagers when they came, so they had to go to school. Of course they are happy to be free, to have food to eat and to wear nice clothes, but they have a hard time fitting in in the south.

Moving from one of the world's poorest countries to one of the richest is not easy.

Big Problems Besides having to learn how to live in a rich, modern country, the teens have many other problems to deal with:

1. Bad health. Because they were starving before, many of them are now sick and weak.
2. Uneducated. Many of them were street children who never went to school, so now they have to attend classes with little kids who are much younger than they are.

HARD WORDS

- **defectors**: people who escape from their country to another country
- **a...death**: a horrible life, like a bad dream
- **to fit in**: to feel like they belong, have friends
- **to deal with**: to solve, to overcome

3. **Feel inferior** Most NK teens are smaller than their South Korean classmates, so they feel inferior.

4. **Feel different** Everybody knows they came from the north, so they aren't completely accepted.

5. **"Too Modern" Lifestyle** They are confused by the rich, modern lifestyle. They never saw cell phones, ATMs, bus fare machines, phone booths, etc., and don't know how to count money.

6. **Lifestyle "Too Fast"** While being very modern, South Korean life is also very busy and competitive. Life in the north is quiet and slow. There are few cars.

7. **Homesickness** It is not easy to leave your home and all of your friends and go to a new place where you don't know anyone. They miss their homes and friends in the north very much.

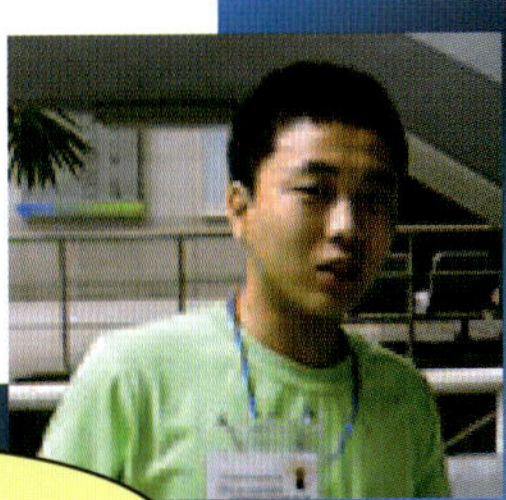

DEFECTOR KANG WON CHUL

There is one thing different about South Korean schools that the defectors hate. In the South, teachers sometimes hit the students. But in North Korea teachers never hit their students.

If North Koreans cannot be made a part of South Korean society, then the society will divide into two classes—a rich class of well-educated South Koreans, and a working class of former North Koreans.

The southerners will live in nice houses and drive nice cars, but the northerners will live in poor areas and ride on bicycles and buses.

HARD WORDS

- **feel inferior**: think that they are not as good as other people
- **(be) accepted**: have other people like them
- **(be) competitive**: always taking tests to get a better job to make more money
- **working class**: poor people who have dirty jobs

PRACTICE

MAKE NEW SENTENCES.

...to fit in

1. She...her new class
2. He...at church
3. They...at school

SHE HAD A HARD TIME **FITTING IN** AT COLLEGE.

...to deal with...

4. Fathers...problems
5. Students...tests
6. Teachers...bad students

TAXI DRIVERS HAVE MANY BAD CUSTOMERS **TO DEAL WITH**.

DISCUSS

ANSWERS ON PAGE 123

1. Why are each of these things problems for teenage defectors? Which is the biggest problem for them? Tell why you think so.
   a. Moving from a quiet, poor life to a busy life in a rich country
   b. Having to go to school with young children
   c. Living in a modern society with cell phones and computers
   d. Being homesick for family and friends in the north
2. If you moved to another country, what would be the biggest problems that you would have? Tell why you think so.
3. Would you like to attend classes with little children who were 6 years younger than you? Why or why not?
4. Are there any North Korean defectors in your school or do you know of any? If so, answer these questions:
   a. Do they have many friends? Do other students treat them differently?
   b. Do you think that they are lonely? Have you tried to become friends with them? Why or why not?
   c. Do they study in the same class as you or in a different class?
5. What are some things that South Korean students can do to make the students from the north feel happy in their new country?
6. Why is it very important for South Koreans to try and make North Koreans fit into southern society? What kind of social problems will occur if that doesn't happen? Tell why or why not.
7. How long (how many years) will it take for today's defectors to feel a part of southern society? Tell why you think so.

UNIT 20

MULTI-CULTURAL KOREA

INTERMARRIAGE

A big change is underway in Korean society. It is fast becoming multi-cultural, and it is happening for two reasons: a) many Korean men are marrying women from outside Korea, and b) foreign workers are now living in Korea and marrying Koreans.

What this means is that Korean society will soon have two social classes—a class of pure Koreans and another class of citizens who are just half Korean. When that happens, Korea will be a multi-cultural country like the USA, Canada, and Australia.

Irreversible trend. This process of changing from a population of pure Koreans to multi-cultural has to happen because Korean men outnumber Korean women. Some of the men must marry a foreigner or not get married at all.

Also, Korea needs the foreign workers to work in its factories. There aren't enough Korean men to work in the factories, so workers from other Asian countries are hired. If the foreigners leave, some factories will have to close.

The country depends on the factories to make the cars and hi-tech products that Korea sells to foreign countries. If the foreign workers left, the Korean economy would be hurt badly.

HARD WORDS

- **intermarriage**: when two people from different countries get married
- **multi-cultural**: a society made up of people from many different countries
- **social classes**: different groups of people in the same society
- **to outnumber**: to be more than the other *(more men than women)*

As long as things stay the same as now, Korea will be multi-cultural by 2025. At first most multiculturals won't look much different from pure Koreans because both parents were Asians.

But they'll be easy to spot because almost all of them will be bi-lingual or better. They will speak Korean plus the language of their other parent and probably English too if their parents spoke to each other in English.

In that case, they may have an easier time finding jobs than Koreans who can speak just Korean and maybe English.

But another thing to think about is how they will be treated by pure Koreans. Koreans put a lot of concern on a person's background, so multinationals will always seem a little different.

What kind of problems will that cause for Korean society? If they are tri-lingual, they may get all of the best jobs, and other Koreans might resent them.

Or will other Koreans dislike them just because they are not 100% Korean? We can't say now, but we will soon find out.

BILINGUAL PEOPLE CAN SPEAK TWO LANGUAGES

HARD WORDS

- **to spot**: to see, be able to know just by looking
- **bi-lingual...better**: can speak two or more languages
- **(be) treated**: whether other people are kind or mean to you
- **to resent**: feel jealous and angry at the same time

PRACTICE

CHOOSE THE CORRECT PREFIX / MAKE NEW SENTENCES

1. She speaks two languages, so she is........-lingual.
2. They speak many languages, so they are........-lingual.
3. My mother speaks just Korean, so she's........-lingual.

A. MONO-
B. BI-
C. MULTI-

...to spot

4. Dogs and cats…crowd
5. Bicycles...busy street
6. Small cars... road

SMALL CHILDREN ARE HARD TO SPOT IN A BIG CROWD OF PEOPLE.

ANSWERS ON PAGE 123

DISCUSS

1. How do you feel about Korea becoming multinational country? Tell why you think so.
   a. I don't like it. I don't want Korea to change.
   b. It's good. Korean society will become more interesting.
2. How will bi-cultural Koreans be treated by the pure Koreans? Tell why you think so.
   a. They will treat them the same as all other Korean people.
   b. They will treat them like foreigners.
3. Will Korea become a multi-lingual society instead of the mono-lingual society that it is now? (just one national language)
4. Do most Koreans realize that Korea is becoming multi-cultural? Will most Koreans like it or not? Why do you think so?
5. Will becoming multinational change the way that Koreans eat? Will Korean food change? Will restaurants serve different kinds of foods or just Korean food? Tell why you think so.
6. Will bi-cultural Koreans have an easier time or a harder time being accepted into the best schools? Tell why you think so.
7. Will bi-cultural Koreans have an easier time or a harder time than other Koreans in finding a job with a famous company? Tell why you think so.
8. Where will bi-cultural Koreans live? Tell why you think so.
   a. They will live in the same places as all other Korean people.
   b. They will live in communities, separate from other Koreans.
9. Will the Korean customs and way of thinking change if Korea becomes multi-cultural? Why or why not?
10. Which group will have an easier time of finding a job—pure Koreans or multinationals who can speak 3 languages fluently? Tell why.

UNIT 21 KOREA'S CAR CRISIS

ELECTRIC CARS

The world is headed for an energy crisis because it is running out of oil. A little of the energy that we use comes from the sun (solar power) or wind power, but most of it comes from burning oil. We use oil to run our cars, buses, trucks, and airplanes, and to heat and cool our buildings.

The energy crisis will hit Korea badly because Korea has to import the oil that it uses from other countries. So what will happen when oil-producing countries have no more oil to sell to Korea? Korea will be in big trouble.

KOREANS LIKE BIG CARS BETTER THAN SMALL CARS

THE E-ZONE ELECTRIC VEHICLE

The Problem The Korean government doesn't plan to wait until that day, so it is trying to change the way that Koreans drive. It is asking Koreans to buy electric cars instead of the big gas guzzlers that they're buying now. Electric cars are now being sold in Korea.

But there is a problem: Koreans like big cars, and electric cars are very small. They also go slow. So will Koreans make the switch to electric cars?

HARD WORDS

- **crisis**: a very serious problem
- **to import**: to buy from other countries
- **gas-guzzlers**: big cars that use a lot of gas
- **make...switch**: to change from one to the other

AN ELECTRIC CAR GETTING A CHARGE ON THE STREET.

Maybe someday big electric cars that go fast will be available, but that day is a long way off. Meanwhile, the price of gas keeps rising, and it will continue to rise as the world's supply of oil continues to decrease.

There is another reason why the price of gas in Korea is rising: Koreans keep using more and more oil. That's because they keep buying bigger and bigger cars. Korean drivers don't seem to be very worried about the energy crisis.

How much for gas? In 2010 Korean drivers were paying 2½ times more for gasoline than in 1997. But that's nothing compared to what may be coming.

Some experts think that the price of oil may rise 250% in the next few years. If that happens Korean drivers will have to pay more than 4,000 won for one liter of gas.

How expensive must gas be before Koreans will switch to smaller cars? We may not have to wait long to find out.

SMALL CARS USE LESS GAS THAN BIG CARS

HARD WORDS

- **a...off**: won't happen for a long time
- **to keep + v**: to continue (doing something)
- **to decrease**: become less than before
- **that's...coming**: may soon be paying even more

PRACTICE

MAKE NEW SENTENCES USING THE WORDS IN GREEN.

...to run out of 1. The store….milk 2. We…rice 3. The printer…paper	HE **RAN OUT OF** MONEY LAST WEEK. 
...to keep +...ing 4. I...cell phone 5. The baby…spoon 6. He...English book	 MY MOTHER **KEEPS LOSING** HER CAR KEYS.

DISCUSS

ANSWERS ON PAGE 123

1. What do you think of electric cars? Tell why you think so.
   a. I think they are good idea.
   b. I think they are too small and will never be popular.
2. What do you think of the Korean government trying to make people buy electric cars? Tell why you think so.
   a. It's a good idea.
   b. It won't work. Koreans will never buy tiny electric cars.
3. What would make Koreans decide to buy electric cars?
   a. ...if they know that the world is running out of oil
   b. ...if gas costs too much
   c. ...only when there isn't any more gas to buy
4. How much money would Koreans be willing to pay for gas before trading in their big cars for small regular cars or electric cars? Tell why you think so.
   a. 3000 won / liter
   b. 5000 won / liter
   c. Whatever gas costs; they will never buy small cars.
5. Do Koreans care about the world running out of oil? Why or why not?
6. What is the main reason why Koreans buy big cars instead of small cars? Tell why you think so.
   a. They need big cars for their big families or for their work.
   b. They want to impress their friends and neighbors.
7. What kind of cars will Koreans be driving in 2020—big or small?

UNIT 22 RECYCLING AND CONSERVATION

The old way It didn't always use to be this way. Before recycling started in Korea during the 1990s, all garbage was mixed together. People who lived in high-rise apartment buildings just dumped the garbage into a chute, and it would pile up high on the first floor.

The piles of garbage smelled bad and attracted insects and rats. Now people who live in those apartments separate their garbage into recycling bins.

WHY RECYCLE?

Just as people do in all advanced countries, Koreans recycle their garbage. Recycling is a part of today's world. The world's natural resources are running out, so everybody has to help save the earth.

Recycle bins When Koreans throw away their garbage, they have to separate it into several different recycling bins. There is usually a bin for glass, another one for cans and other metal items, a bin for plastics, one for paper, and a large container for wet garbage.

A BIG PILE OF SMELLY GARBAGE

HARD WORDS

- **natural resources**: water, oil, air, etc.
- **to run out**: use it all, there will be no more
- **hi-rise**: a building higher than 9 floors
- **chute**: like an elevator shaft for garbage
- **pile up**: make a pile, (like a little hill)

There are many benefits of recycling:

1. **Recycling saves energy.** The most important benefit is that recycled material can be used again. Recycling reduces the amount of energy needed to produce the same item again by 80 to 95%.

2. **Recycling saves the earth.** When garbage decomposes, it produces a gas called methane. Methane gas contributes to global warming. Recycling reduces the amount of methane gas going into the atmosphere.

3. **Recycling preserves natural resources.** Making paper and cardboard means cutting down trees. That's not good because trees make the oxygen we need to breathe. Making plastic uses oil, and we are running out of oil.

EVERYBODY MUST RECYCLE

Every piece of garbage that we throw away either contributes to global warming or uses up valuable natural resources. That should be enough reason to convince everyone that they need to recycle.

HARD WORDS

- **benefits**: good results
- **to decompose**: to break apart
- **atmosphere**: the layer of air around the earth
- **to convince**: make them agree
- **to reuse**: to fill it up with water again
- **harmful chemicals**: can hurt the body

Plastic water bottles

Have you ever noticed the triangle that is stamped on the bottom of a plastic water bottle? If it looks like this with a "1" inside, do NOT reuse it. This kind of plastic should be used only ONCE because after some time it leaks harmful chemicals into the water.

PRACTICE

MAKE NEW SENTENCES USING THE WORDS IN GREEN.

...to pile up 1. My homework...desk (on) 2. Snow...front door (at) 3. Their money...bank (in)	GARBAGE **PILED UP** IN THE STREET. 
...to use up 4. He...gas...car 5. Breakfast...eggs...kitchen 6. They...water...can	 I **USED UP** ALL OF THE MONEY IN MY POCKETS.

ANSWERS ON PAGE 123

DISCUSS

1. How important is it for people to recycle? Tell why you think so.
   a. It is very important.
   b. It's just a little important. Other things are more important.
2. How can recycling save energy?
3. How does recycling help save the earth's natural resources?
4. Why do most Korean people recycle? Tell why you think so.
   a. They do it because they have to (It's the law).
   b. They do it because they want to save the earth.
5. Which of these things are bad for the environment and which are not? Tell why you think so.
   a. paper bags and boxes
   b. plastic bags and bottles
   c. spoiled food
   d. old cell phones
   e. used batteries
   f. rotten fruit and vegetables
6. What is the reason why some people don't want to recycle? Tell why you think so.
   a. They don't understand why recycling is important.
   b. They are lazy and don't care about saving the earth.
7. What is the best way to make people not throw garbage along roads and highways? Tell why you think so.
8. How should people who throw garbage into the streets be punished? Tell why you think so.
9. What is the best way to reduce the amount of garbage that we throw away? Do you do those things?

UNIT 23 WORLD POPULATION

because people didn't live very long. A hundred years ago people only lived about 50 years.

But today, because of modern science and medical advances, people are living into their 80s or 90s. Scientists are working hard to find new ways of producing food to feed a growing number of people.

FOOD PRODUCTION

There are now almost 7 billion people in the world, and by the year 2025 the world's population will probably double.

Every year there are 85 million more people than the year before. The population is increasing by 1.7% a year. So for every 1,000 people on the earth today there will be 1,017 this time next year.

Can the earth support that many people? Will there be enough food for everyone? Before the last century people didn't worry about the increase of the world's population

WILL THERE BE ENOUGH FOOD FOR EVERYBODY?

HARD WORDS

- **to double**: to become 2 times more
- **this...year**: one year from today
- **to support**: have enough food and water for everyone
- **advances**: new discoveries
- **into...90s**: 80 or 90 years old or more

But the news is not all bad. Since 2000 the rate of increase has been going down. And if it continues until 2050, the world's population will start to fall.

Korea is one of the countries where not enough babies are being born. If Korean families don't start having more children soon, Korea's population will start to shrink by 2020. So the Korean government gives tax breaks to couples that have more than 2 children.

But some countries like India and China have the opposite problem—too many babies. So China has a 1-child policy. The government asks couples to have just one child. For each child more than one, the couple has to pay more tax.

ONE CHILD PER FAMILY IN CHINA

Many people think that overpopulation isn't anything to worry about because a lot of the world's land isn't being used. In some places like North and South America, only 25% of the land is being used for farmland, living areas, and roads. The other 75% of the land is vacant.

SO MUCH VACANT LAND

HARD WORDS

- **rate...increase**: how fast it is going up
- **shrink**: become smaller, less
- **tax breaks**: pay less tax
- **vacant**: not being used for anything

PRACTICE

MAKE NEW SENTENCES USING THE WORDS IN GREEN.

Cell phones **will be a lot** less expensive **this time next year**.

1. THE INTERNET...FASTER
2. PRICES OF LCD TVS...CHEAPER
3. GASOLINE...MORE EXPENSIVE

1. ______________________________________
2. ______________________________________
3. ______________________________________

ANSWERS ON PAGE 124

DISCUSS

1. Is world population growth something we need to worry about? Why or why not?
2. Do you think that making families that have more children pay less tax is a good idea? Why or why not?
3. Why is Korea close to having a shrinking population? Why are Koreans having fewer children than before?
4. Why is it important to have a growing population instead of a shrinking population? What kinds of problems will occur if Korea's population shrinks too much?
5. Is it okay for the Chinese government to tax families more if they have too many children? Why or why not?
6. Population is increasing faster in poor countries than in rich countries. Why do people in poor countries have more children?
7. Many problems occur in cities that become overcrowded with too many people. Which of these is the biggest problem?

   a. crimes (all kinds)
   b. air pollution
   c. traffic jams
   d. food shortage
   e. lack of clean water
   f. too much noise

8. Do you think the world will ever run out of food? Why or why not?
9. Why is much of the vacant land in the world no guarantee that the world will never run out of food? (These are pictures of some vacant land.)

10. How can recycling and conservation help prevent a worldwide food shortage ? Tell why you think so.

UNIT 24

FAST FOOD

BURGERS AND PIZZA

There are a lot of western-style fast food restaurants in Korea where hamburgers, pizza, fried chicken, donuts, and ice cream are sold.

The most popular fast food restaurants in Korea are foreign-owned chain restaurants. The first ones that opened here were McDonalds and Burger King in 1987, just in time for the '88 Olympics.

They were soon followed by Pizza Hut, Dunkin' Donuts, Wendy's, Winchell's Donuts, KFC, Dairy Queen and Lotteria.

Fast food restaurants can now be found in cities and towns all over Korea. They can even be found inside shopping malls and department stores.

As Koreans' taste for fast food has increased, so has their weight. Before fast food Koreans were thinner than they are today. That's because almost all fast food contains either too much fat, too much sugar, or too much of both.

HARD WORDS

- **chain restaurant**: restaurant companies that have branches in several locations
- **taste...weight**: Koreans got fatter because of eating fast food
- **Before...food**: ...before there were any fast food restaurants in Korea

WHO DOESN'T LOVE DONUTS?

There are fast food restaurants all over Korea now so it is hard to imagine that before 1988 there weren't any at all.

Fast food restaurants are where today's Korean high school and middle school kids meet their friends. They can't imagine a world without fast food restaurants.

People like fast food restaurants because they're self-service. There are no waiters or waitresses to bother you or ask you to leave. So it's possible to sit at a table for as long as you want with just one drink. That's not possible in a sit-down restaurant. You have to leave after you finish eating.

Unfortunately, there's one problem with fast food: it's not good for you. People who eat a lot of hamburgers, donuts and fried chicken get fat.

Fast food isn't nutritious, but we eat it anyway. We know it makes people fat, but we can't stop eating it. Why not? Because it tastes too good!

THESE KIDS EAT TOO MUCH FAST FOOD

HARD WORDS

- **a...without**: a place when there isn't any
- **sit...restaurant**: one with waiters or waitresses
- **(be) not...you**: bad for the body
- **nutritious**: contains vitamins and minerals

PRACTICE

MAKE NEW SENTENCES USING THE WORDS IN GREEN.

...(be) just in time 1. She...watch the TV program. 2. He...see the team win. 3. I...eat dinner with the family.	I ARRIVED JUST IN TIME TO TAKE THE TEST. 
...a...?... without 4. She...time...cell phones 5. He... world...email 6. We…life...the Internet	 I CAN'T IMAGINE A WORLD WITHOUT TV.

ANSWERS ON PAGE 124

DISCUSS

1. How often do you eat fast food? What's your favorite kind of fast food and why?
2. Do you sometimes hang out with your friends at fast food restaurants? If there were no fast food restaurants where would you go to meet your friends?
3. How many of these fast food chain restaurants do you know? What kinds of foods do they sell? Which ones do you eat the most often?
4. When you eat fast food do you ever think about whether it is good for you? Do you care about your health? Why or why not?
5. Why do children and teenagers like fast food so much more than their parents do? Tell why you think so.
6. Which of these Korean fast foods do you eat often? Which ones are nutritious and which are not?

7. Why are fast foods less nutritious than the food that you order at a sit-down restaurant? Why can't they make fast food nutritious?
8. Which of these meals would you rather eat if you were hungry after school and why?

UNIT 25 DEADLY CIGARETTES

LITTLE BOYS LEARNING TO SMOKE

GETTING HOOKED

More and more teenagers are starting to smoke at a time when more and more adults are quitting. These teenagers who smoke aren't very smart because they should realize that something must be wrong. There has to be a reason why adults are giving up cigarettes, and the reason must be bad. People don't stop doing something for no reason at all.

Kids begin smoking for three main reasons—curiosity (wanting to see what it's like), desire to be grown up (it's what big people do), and thinking that their bodies are strong enough to handle it even if it's dangerous.

They feel that they have a very long life ahead of them and that nothing will happen. They think they can't get sick. But by the time they realize the truth, it's too late. They're already hooked on cigarettes.

HARD WORDS

- **to realize**: suddenly have a clear understanding of it
- **to give up**: stop doing something
- **to handle it**: to endure it, to take care of the problem easily
- **(be) hooked**: addicted, the body needs to have it , can't stop doing it

SMOKING MAKES TEETH TURN YELLOW.

Teenagers are impatient. They are tired of being kids, and they want to be adults...fast. They think that the way to be an adult fast is to smoke cigarettes.

That's too bad because smoking cigarettes is about the worst thing a person could do with his or her body. It is the only product sold that causes death when used properly.

The problem is that kids and teenagers think their bodies are too strong to be harmed. Or they also think that they will be able to stop anytime they want.

That's too bad because cigarettes contain nicotine, and nicotine is addictive. If the body gets it enough times, it starts to need it. That's why smokers can't stop. Their bodies need the nicotine.

About half of today's teenage smokers will die of cancer or another disease caused by smoking.

Also, smoking is a dirty habit, bad for both the world and for our lungs. It also makes teeth turn yellow and gives a smoker bad breath.

SMOKING IS A DIRTY HABIT.

HARD WORDS

- **(be) tired of**: don't want to do it anymore because it's boring or unpleasant
- **the...properly**: It can cause a person to get cancer and die.
- **(be) addictive**: makes the body depend on it
- **habit**: something that you do all the time
- **to give...bad breath**: make a person's mouth smell bad

PRACTICE

MAKE NEW SENTENCES USING THE WORDS IN GREEN.

...to give up 1. She...swimming...18 2. He...playing baseball...35 3. He...stealing...arrested	I GAVE UP PLAYING THE PIANO WHEN I WAS 15. 
...to handle 4. She...new English class 5. He...all of the homework 6. We...the long 12-hour drive	 I COULDN'T HANDLE A WORLD WITHOUT CARS.

ANSWERS ON PAGE 124

DISCUSS

1. How do you feel about smoking? Tell why you think so.
   a. It's bad for you. People shouldn't smoke cigarettes.
   b. It's okay. People can smoke if they want to.
2. Which of these are important reasons not to smoke cigarettes? Discuss each one.
   a. Teenagers shouldn't smoke.
   b. It makes your lungs black.
   c. It causes cancer.
   d. It makes the teeth turn yellow.
   e. It gives you bad breath.
   f. It's bad for the environment.
3. What is your opinion of teenagers who smoke? Are they all bad kids, or do some good kids smoke too? Tell why you think so.
4. What percentage of students in your school smokes cigarettes? How do you know it? Where do the students smoke?
5. Is it possible to be a good student but also smoke cigarettes? Do some good students smoke, or are all smokers bad students?
6. Why do you think that most teenage smokers decided to start smoking?
   a. They wanted to look older.
   b. They like to do dangerous things.
   c. Another reason.
7. Are there any teenage gang members who do not smoke cigarettes? If not, why not?
8. Is it okay for everyone over 21 to smoke? Why or why not?

HOW BAD IS THIS?

UNIT 26 LIFE IN THE 21ST CENTURY

We know that will happen because our technology is improving very rapidly. Not long ago two of the things that we now take for granted didn't even exist: mobile phones, and the Internet.

The Internet, which was first called the world wide web, wasn't invented until 1992, and the world didn't start using it until 1995. That's when Windows first included a web browser. By 2000 the Internet had become a necessity of life.

A HI-TECH FUTURE

Nobody knows for sure what the world will look like 20 or 25 years from now, but we can be sure that it will be high-tech. The gadgets we use today, like cars, computers, and phones, will look a lot different from the way they look now. Our homes will look different, and we will use many hi-tech devices that haven't even been invented yet.

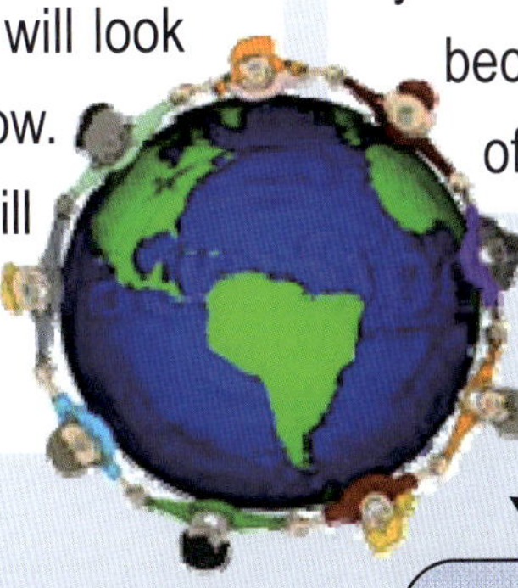

BY 2000 THE INTERNET WAS NECESSARY FOR LIFE

HARD WORDS

- **gadgets**: electrical or mechanical tools
- **hi-tech devices**: computers, cell phones, etc.
- **to...granted**: to expect to have something to use, cannot imagine not having it
- **wasn't...1992**: same as, "it was invented in 1992."
- **web browser**: software program that lets you use the Internet

The four most used hi-tech tools being used today are cell phones, computers, video calling, and flat-screen TVs. It would be hard to live without these things.

Wireless phones. Cell phones of the future will be more than just something for making a call, listening to MP3, or playing a game.

Your cell phone number will be your personal I.D. number that will never change. Every person will have one, and there won't be any more landline telephones.

Video calling. Video phone calling will soon be done from your cell phone. We also won't have paper books anymore; we will read books electronically.

WE WILL READ BOOKS ON A WIRELESS DEVICE

HARD WORDS

- **wireless**: like cell phones, have no wires
- **to make...call**: to telephone someone
- **landline phones**: phones in buildings
- **electronically**: through the Internet

Computers and Flat Screen TVs. We now have big LCD and LED TVs that can be hung on a wall, but soon screens will cover the walls.

At the same time, computers will get smaller and smaller. Already hand-held computers are being used.

HANDHELD COMPUTER

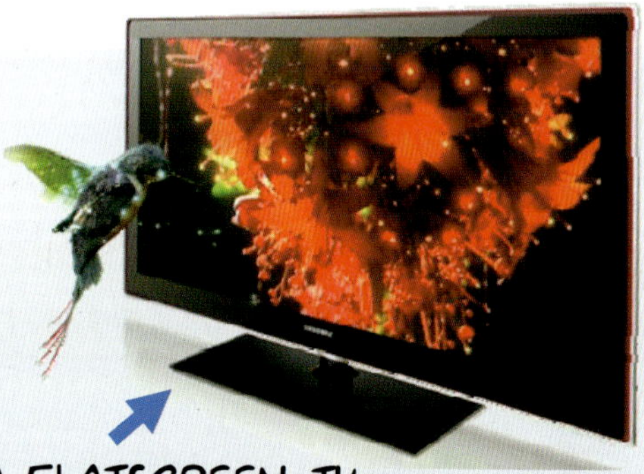

LED FLATSCREEN TV

FLAT SCREEN TVs WILL SOON COVER ENTIRE WALLS.

PRACTICE

WRITE SENTENCES CHANGING THE WORDS IN BLUE.

The Internet wasn't invented until the 1990s.

1. TVs...SOLD IN KOREA...THE 1970s.
2. TELEPHONES...USED BY MOST PEOPLE...1920s.
3. OUR SCHOOL...BUILT...1999.

1920s PHONE

1. --
2. --
3. --

ANSWERS ON PAGE 124

DISCUSS

1. Could you live without any of these hi-tech tools? Could you be happy if you didn't have them? Why or why not?
   a. cell phone
   b. computer
   c. flat screen TV
   d. MP3 player
   e. DVD player
   f. the Internet
2. Which kind of book would you rather read—a paper book or a book on a hand-held computer? Why?
3. Have you ever made a video phone call over the Internet? What is the best thing about making video calls instead of regular calls?
4. Would you like it if the caller could see your face every time you talk on the phone? Why or why not?
5. How did people communicate with one another before the Internet? How did the Internet make communicating more convenient?
6. Should students be allowed to carry hand-held computers into the classroom? Why or why not?
7. Which of these has changed the most in the past 15 years?
   a. TVs
   b. telephones
   c. computers
   d. music-listening devices
8. Would you like to have a computer small enough to carry in your pocket? Why or why not?
9. Should students be allowed to use their cell phones and computers in the classroom? Why or why not?
10. Which of these do you think will change the most in the next 20 years? Tell why you think so.
    a. Computers
    b. Cell phones
    c. The Internet
    d. CDs and DVDs

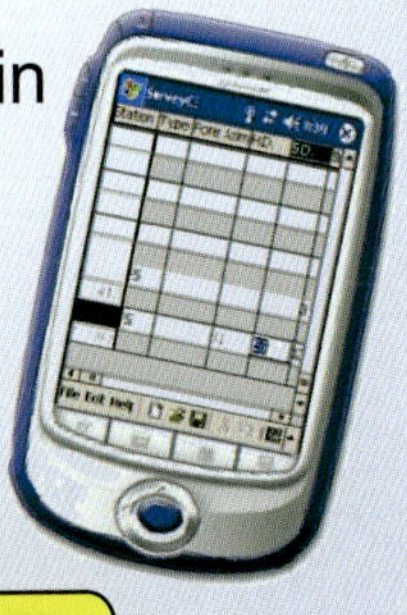

A POCKET COMPUTER

UNIT 27 CELLULAR PHONES

Almost nobody had a cell phone before 2000. Some businessmen were using them, but their cell phones were nothing like the ones we use today.

1995 MOBILE PHONE

They were too big to carry in a pocket, and they were very heavy. They also didn't work very well. Sometimes you couldn't hear the other person talking or they couldn't hear you.

LIFECHANGERS

Nothing has changed the way that we communicate on the personal level more than the cell phone. Almost everyone has one. We depend on them in our daily lives, and our lives would become more difficult if we didn't have them. The amazing thing is that we've only had them since around 2000. In just a few years, they became essential items in our lives.

1988 WIRELESS PHONE

HARD WORDS

- **communicate...level**: speak with friends and family
- **essential items**: can't live without them
- **nothing...today**: The ones of today are much better.

Before cell phone there were pagers ("beepers"), which you could call by phone but you couldn't talk to the person. That person would see your phone number on the pager and call you back from a telephone.

Missed meetings Before pagers, missed appointments were a part of life. It was hard to set a time to meet a friend because traffic jams usually made people late.

There was no way to tell your friend that you were stuck in traffic and would be late. The person waiting would get tired of waiting and go home. When you finally arrived, your friend was already gone.

No more angry friends. Today such a thing is almost impossible because everybody has a cell phone. All we have to do is to call our friend and tell them to wait. No one gets angry. Cell phones are lifesavers.

Cell phones have changed a lot in a very short time, and they will change even more. The next cell phones will not have any push buttons. They will all be "touch-screen" and very light.

HARD WORDS

- **a...life**: happened every day, all the time
- **traffic jams**: when cars can't move
- **stuck...traffic**: no way to escape
- **get tired of**: don't want to do it anymore, boring
- **lifesaver**: something that makes living much easier

PRACTICE

MAKE NEW SENTENCES USING THE WORDS IN BLUE.

to get tired of...

1. She...watching...TV show
2. He...studying...subject
3. They...wearing...uniform

I GOT TIRED OF EATING THE SAME THING EVERY DAY.

to wonder...

4. I...computers...use
5. I...cars...drive
6. I...TVs...watch

I WONDER WHAT KIND OF PHONE WE'LL BE USING 5 YEARS FROM NOW.

DISCUSS

ANSWERS ON PAGE 124

1. Do you have a cell phone? If so, how long have you had it? Why did you get it (main reason)?
2. How would our lives change if we couldn't use our cell phones anymore?
3. How many people in your family have cell phones? Who uses their phone the most and how (for what reason) do they use it?
4. From what age should a person own a cell phone? For example, should an 8-year-old child have a cell phone? Why or why not?
5. What are some ways in which a cell phone is better than a regular landline phone?
6. If you had to give up all of these devices and *keep just one*, which one would you choose to keep and why?
   a. cell phone
   b. computer
   c. MP3 player
   d. the Internet →

7. When buying a new cell phone, which of these things are important to you and which are not? Tell why.
   a. make and receive calls
   b. send text messages
   c. listen to music
   d. play games
   e. watch movies
   f. use the Internet
8. What should be done with cell phones after they get old? Should you just throw them away? Why or why not?
9. How often should a person change his or her cell phone? Tell why you think so.
10. Should students be allowed to carry cell phones into the classroom? Why or why not?

UNIT 28

THE NEW ANIMATION

Cloudy With A Chance of Meatballs (2009)

No longer do artists have to draw and paint each frame of a cartoon by hand. Now it's all done on computers, and the images don't look drawn. They look real.

CGI animation attracts many more people than the old animation movies did. Only children would want to watch a movie like "Cinderella", but adults are just as fascinated by CGI films as children are.

Today's animation films aren't just for little kids; they are mainstream movies.

C.G.I.

Thanks to computers, animation has been re-invented. Today's animation is 100 times better than the first Mickey Mouse cartoon in 1928. It's called C.G.I. for computer-generated imagery.

WALT DISNEY'S STEAMBOAT WILLIE (1928) →

Ratatouille (2007)

HARD WORDS

- **frame**: movies are made of thousands of small pictures (frames) on a roll of film. CGI is digital, not filmed with cameras
- **to...real**: look almost like real people
- **to attract**: to be liked by a lot of people
- **(be) fascinated (by)**: to be amazed by
- **mainstream movies**: movies that everybody wants to see

It's easy to figure out why CGI animation movies are now mainstream: the scenery and characters look almost human because they are 3-D, not 2-dimensional like the older cartoon characters.

The audience can identify with the characters because they seem real, but they can also do things that real people could never do, such as fly.

A good example of humans or near-humans doing the impossible was 2009's Avatar. In that movie both the characters and their planet were computer-generated. They even had their own language, invented for them just for the movie.

Walt Disney's "UP" (2009)

CGI has a bright future because the technology keeps improving. The characters are getting more and more humanlike and the locations more amazing. Many people think that CGI animation will someday replace human actors.

"Little Mermaid" (1989)

2-DIMENSIONAL HAND-DRAWN

"The Incredibles" (2004)

3-D CGI

In some ways CGI characters are better than human actors. They don't get sick, never come to work late, never get tired, and they work for free.

HARD WORDS

- **3-D**: 3 dimensional: height, width, and depth →

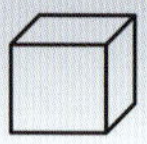

- **to...with**: to feel that they are people like us
- **humanlike**: to look like a half human and half cartoon character, but behave, talk, and think like a human →
- **someday...actors**: all movies will be made on computers with CGI, no use of film, cameras, and human actors.

"Monster House" (2006)

PRACTICE

CGI, DRAWN, OR REAL???

1

2

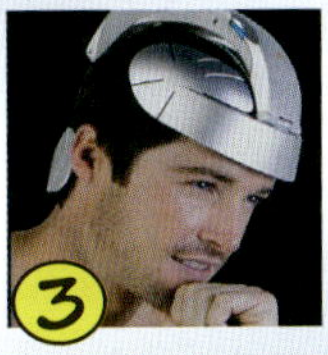
3

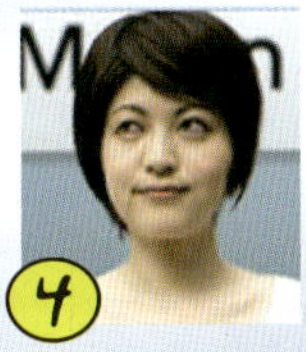
4

5

6

For each image choose:

a. hand-drawn
b. CGI
c. real person

1 - - - - -
2 - - - - -
3 - - - - -
4 - - - - -
5 - - - - -
6 - - - - -

ANSWERS ON PAGE 124

DISCUSS

1. Do you like animation movies? Why or why not?
2. Which type of animation would you rather watch—hand-drawn or CGI? Why do you prefer that kind?
3. Do you have a Playstation or X-Box? Would those games be just as much fun without CGI? Why or why not?
4. Will CGI characters someday replace all human actors in movies? Why or why not?
5. What are some advantages of making movies with CGI characters?
6. What are some problems with making movies with human actors? (What problems do they cause that CGI characters don't?)
7. If all movies were made with CGI…
   a. Would you be interested in seeing the movies?
   b. Would the films be more interesting than films with human actors?
   c. Would you cry if the movie were sad?
8. In the movie, "Avatar", a new language was invented for the characters in the movie. How long would it take to create a language, and why would movie producers do it just for a movie?
9. Which kind of action movies do you prefer—normal ones with no CGI or CGI animations like Harry Potter or Lord of the Rings? Tell why.
10. Will there be movies 100 years from now or will they fade in popularity?

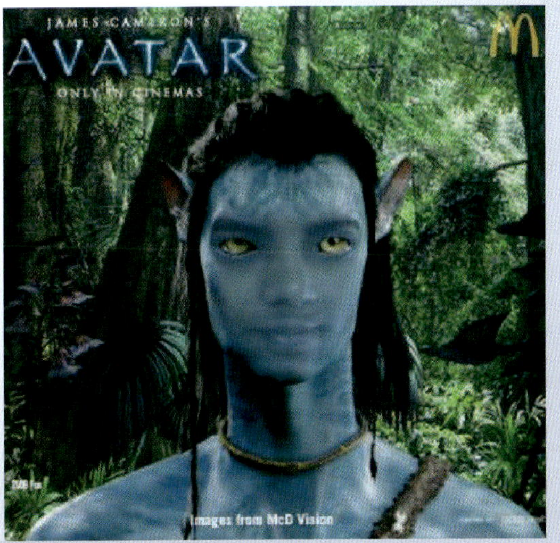

UNIT 29 SPACE EXPLORATION

A KOREAN-MADE ROCKET TAKES OFF FROM NARO SPACE CENTER

SPACE PROGRAM

The Korea Aerospace Research Institute (KARI) wants South Korea to be one of the world's top 10 aerospace powers by 2015. Most Koreans don't even know that their country has a space program.

It does, and it began in 1987. Now Korea is close to becoming one of the world's top 10 countries in space.

KARI launched its first experimental satellite in 1992. Three years after that they launched a telecommunications satellite called Koreasat One.

Korea became just the 23rd country in the world to have its own commercial satellite.

KOREA'S FIRST SPACE ROCKET LAUNCHED AUGUST 2009

HARD WORDS

- **aerospace power**: a world leader in space exploration
- **experimental**: testing to see if it can be successful
- **satellite**: flies around the earth in space
- **telecommunications**: used for cable TV, Internet, etc.
- **commercial**: communications companies pay money to use it

No country can be an aerospace power without having its own space center so KARI opened its Naro Space Center in Chollanamdo in 2008. It cost more than 265 billion won to build.

When Naro was opened, Korea became just the 13th country in the world to have a launch platform to send rockets into space.

Before Naro was opened, KARI used launch pads in foreign countries to send its satellites into orbit, but doing that was very expensive. It cost even more than what it cost to build Naro.

A SATELLITE IN ORBIT ABOVE THE EARTH

Not all Koreans are pleased with the country's space program. Some people think it's a big waste of money. They say that the money used to build rockets and launch pads could be put to better use such as improving the country's system of roads and highways.

Unfortunately, Korean weather is not ideal for operating a space center. Rockets can't take off in cold temperatures or bad weather, and Korea has plenty of both.

LAUNCHES NEED CLEAR SKIES AND WARM TEMPERATURES

HARD WORDS

- **launch platform**: place where rockets take off
- **into orbit**: to circle around the earth in space
- **put...use**: spend the money on more important things
- **(be) not ideal**: not perfect, in fact, a little bad

PRACTICE

MAKE NEW SENTENCES USING THE WORDS IN BLUE.

to put to better use 1. Her teaching skills... 2. Too much food... 3. The students' time...	THE MONEY IS BEING WASTED. IT COULD BE PUT TO BETTER USE. 
to be ideal 4. His tiny car...taking long trips 5. Your clothes...cold weather 6. My small house...big parties	 KOREA'S WEATHER IS LESS THAN IDEAL FOR ROCKET LAUNCHES.

DISCUSS

ANSWERS ON PAGE 124

1. Is it important for Korea to have a space program? Why or why not?
2. Is it important for every country in the world to have a space program? Why or why not?
3. Is it important whether or not Korea is one of the top 10 aerospace powers by 2015? Why or why not?
4. What is your opinion of Korea going into space? Tell why you think so.
   a. I think it's great.
   b. I don't care about that.
   c. It's a waste of money. Korea should spend its money on more important things.

5. What kind of person becomes an astronaut? What skills do they have to have?
6. Would you like to be an astronaut? Why or why not?
7. Should astronauts be only men, or should there be women astronauts too? Tell why you think so.
8. What should be the purpose of Korea's space program? Tell why you think so.
   a. Put communication satellites into orbit for Korea's use.
   b. Make and sell satellites to other countries.
   c. Send Korean astronauts to the moon and other planets.
9. Should Korea build a space shuttle like the USA's? Why or why not?
10. Rockets can't be launched in Korea's cold or rainy weather, so should the space program be cancelled? Why or why not?

UNIT 30 COMPUTER LEARNING

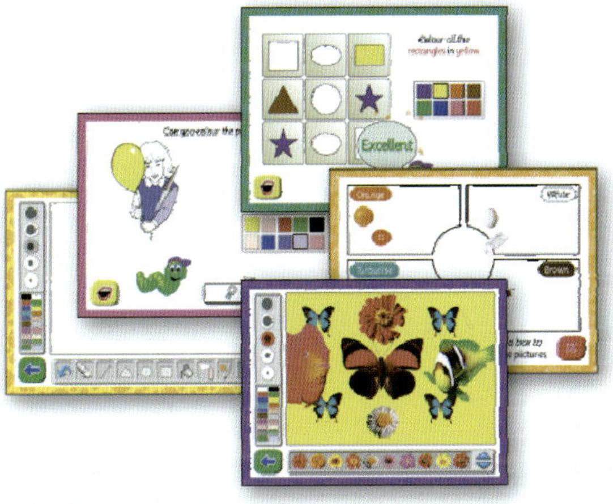

SOFTWARE

Nowadays most high school kids are using computers. These smart kids know that life in the 21st century a person's chances of success may depend on his or her ability to use one.

Starting young Most of today's high school students started using computers when they were in elementary school. In those days most computer programs were games. But now there is a lot of educational software on CD-ROM for students of all ages from elementary school through high school.

Today there are learning programs for math, science, English, and many other subjects. There is even software for toddlers and pre-school kids who can't read yet.

LEARNING WITH COMPUTERS IS FUN

HARD WORDS

- **chances...one**: only people who can use a computer will get good jobs.
- **software**: computer programs that you can buy or download
- **toddlers**: small children ages 2- 3 years old
- **pre-school**: children around 4-5 years old

Teaching spelling. Can you choose the correct answers?
1. When does the sun rise?
2. When does the moon shine brightly?

Educational software makes learning easier than ever before. And since most kids like to play with computers anyway it's a fun way to learn. Learning with computers is more fun than learning from books.

The computers sold in the stores today are multimedia computers, which means that they can also play sounds and show videos and animation. So today's computers are more like teachers than books. The result is that students learn better and faster when they use computers.

But books have one big advantage over computers: you can carry them with you on the subway or on the bus. That lets you study on your way to school.

Of course, there are notebook computers, but they are expensive, and they break easily. They are also too heavy to carry around.

LEARNING HANGUL USING SOFTWARE MAKES IT EASIER.

HARD WORDS

- **multimedia**: sounds, pictures, videos
- **animation**: moving pictures like cartoons
- **advantage...computers**: better than computers

PRACTICE

WRITE SENTENCES FOLLOWING THE EXAMPLE.

Today's computers are more like teachers than books.

1. CELL PHONES...COMPUTERS...TELEPHONES
2. WIDE-SCREEN TVs...MOVIES...TELEVISIONS
3. BIG SUVs...TRUCKS...CARS

1. ______________________________________
2. ______________________________________
3. ______________________________________

ANSWERS ON PAGE 124

DISCUSS

1. Do you have a computer? If so, answer these questions.
   a. How long have you had it?
   b. What do you use it for? What do you do with it?
   c. Who decided to buy it—you or your parents?
2. Do you think that knowing how to use a computer will be necessary for everyone in the 21st century? Why do you think so?
3. For which of the following jobs is knowing how to use a computer the most necessary? (choose more than one) Tell why you think so.
   a. teacher
   b. doctor
   c. salesman
   d. scientist
   e. airline pilot
   f. store clerk
   g. secretary
   h. policeman
   i. musician
4. Do you have any educational software? If so, what kind do you have?
5. What do you think of people who cannot use a computer? Are they lazy or dumb? Tell why you think so.

6. Do you agree that learning with computers is more fun than learning with books? Why or why not?
7. At what age should a person start learning to use a computer? Tell why you think so.
8. Do you think that educational software will ever replace books and teachers? Why or why not?
9. Which of these subjects are well suited to computer learning and which are not? Tell why you think so.
   a. foreign language
   b. mathematics
   c. science
   d. history
   e. cooking
   f. music
   g. reading
   h. geography
   i. sex education

UNIT 31 THE INTERNET

BROADBAND

Most kids use the Internet today, but they don't realize that it is very new. It has only <u>been around</u> since the mid-1990s. At that time it was called the World Wide Web.

Slow connections. Before 2000 the Internet was hard to use because it was very slow and you had to sign in every time. Connecting to the Internet was done through a modem connected to the telephone line. The modem dialed the telephone number of the Internet Service Provider (ISP), and then you typed in your name and password.

But as more and more people began using the Internet the servers, the connection speed slowed down. Sometimes it took 45 seconds <u>to load</u> just one webpage.

Until <u>broadband</u> became available, using the Internet was a <u>frustrating</u> experience.

HARD WORDS

- **be around**: be in existence
- **to load**: download, to see the page on your computer
- **broadband**: very fast connections like ADSL
- **frustrating**: makes you tired and angry

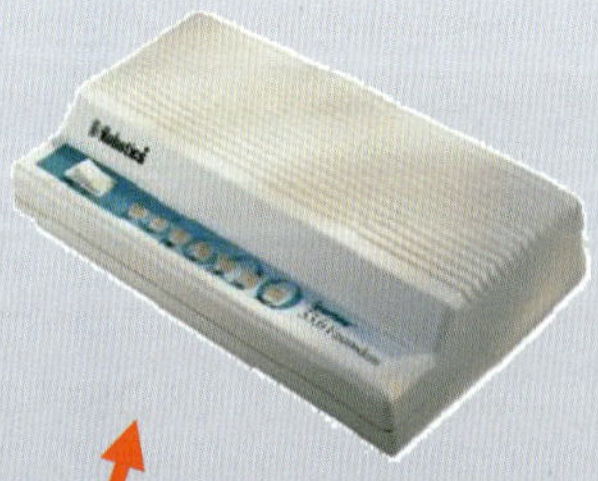

A DIAL-UP MODEM

Because connections were slow, multimedia was not possible. Listening to music and watching videos was out of the question. Almost none of the things that we do today were possible in 2000.

But by 2006 we were downloading music, watching TV, and making video calls with Skype on the Internet. That is all thanks to broadband.

THIS IS HOW WEBSITES LOOKED IN THE 1990S.

VIDEO CALLING WAS MADE POSSIBLE BY BROADBAND

Although the Internet has improved a lot since 1999, it has also become more complicated and more dangerous.

When the Internet was simple, computers didn't need protection against viruses. And before online shopping, hackers couldn't steal any credit card numbers. Now we have to worry about both.

HARD WORDS

- **multimedia**: sounds, pictures, videos
- **(be) out...question**: completely impossible
- **(be) thanks to**: only possible because of
- **viruses**: small programs that destroy information on the computer's hard drive
- **hackers**: computer experts who steal information

PRACTICE

MAKE NEW SENTENCES USING THE WORDS IN BLUE.

to be thanks to... 1. His new car...his getting a job 2. Schools were closed...the snow. 3. My new bicycle...Santa Claus	VIDEO CALLING IS THANKS TO FAST CONNECTIONS. 
to be out of the question 4. Eating ice cream for breakfast… 5. Going hiking on a school day… 6. Wearing shorts to class...	 DYING YOUR HAIR BLUE IS OUT OF THE QUESTION.

DISCUSS

ANSWERS ON PAGE 124

1. Do you use the Internet? If so, answer these questions.
   a. How long have you been using it?
   b. How do you use the Internet? What do you do on there?
   c. Where did you learn how to use the Internet? Who taught you?
2. Which would you rather send—an email or a letter? Why?
3. Is it important to know English to use the Internet or is just Korean enough? Why or why not?
4. How can you protect your computer from getting a computer virus?
5. How should hackers who steal credit card numbers be punished? Tell why you think so.
6. How much has the Internet changed since you were a little kid? What things can we do now that Internet users couldn't do 10 years ago?

7. At what age should children be taught to use a computer? Tell why you think so.
8. How important is it for children to learn how to use the Internet? Tell why you think so.
   a. It's very important.
   b. It's just a little important.
   c. Children don't have to learn about the Internet.
9. How important is it for high school kids to know how to use the Internet? Will it be possible to get a good job without knowing how to use the Internet? If so, what kind of jobs?
10. Would you like to live in a world without any Internet? Why or why not?

UNIT 32 FASHION AWARENESS

LUXURY GENERATION

Seoul's Apgujeong-dong and Cheongdam-dong, where Korea's young people like to hang out, are full of designer brand boutiques like Prada, Gucci, and Louis Vuitton. Today 66% of Korean university students own designer brand items.

Younger buyers Until now most people who bought designer goods were over 30 years old, but today younger Koreans are buying them.

The percentage of people in their 20s who buy designer labels is increasing. At the same time, the percentage of people over 30 who are buying designer brands is falling.

Credit card debt This new desire for designer labels is causing a lot of problems for young Koreans. They don't have money, so they use credit cards instead. They end up with a lot of credit card debt that they can't pay off.

Why do young people buy things they can't pay for? Because all their friends have designer labels, and they want to have the same things too.

HARD WORDS

- **hang out**: spend time with (friends)
- **boutique**: store that sells designer goods
- **people...20s**: between 20 and 29 years old
- **end...with**: the result is...
- **to pay off**: pay it all, don't owe any more

A BOUTIQUE IN SEOUL

Luxury generation. It may be hard to believe, but some parents buy these expensive things for their sons and daughters. These kids are called the "luxury generation".

The main reason why they want designer label goods is to show off. They want their friends to think that they are rich.

Some young people who have jobs will spend their entire monthly salaries on designer goods just so they can impress their friends

Internet sales There are many Internet websites that sell used European designer label goods. The people who buy used items can't afford the prices of new ones sold in Korea.

Designer goods can be very expensive. A woman's purse can cost as much as 2,500,000 won on the Internet and even more if bought in a store.

HANDBAG
₩649,000

MAN'S SHIRT
₩639,000

WHO'S BUYING IT?

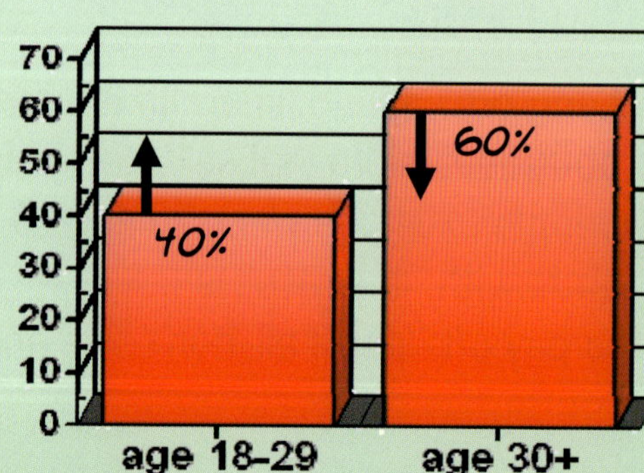

HARD WORDS

- **to show off**: try to make them jealous
- **monthly salary**: all of the money earned working for one month
- **can't afford**: don't have enough money to buy it

PRACTICE

MAKE NEW SENTENCES USING THE WORDS IN GREEN.

...to hang out with friends 1. She....at the library 2. They…on weekends 3. He...at the gym	I USUALLY HANG OUT WITH MY FRIENDS AT MCDONALD'S.
...to end up with 4. She...trouble 5. They...homework 6. My brother...problems	 MY DAD ENDED UP WITH MORE MONEY THAN HE EXPECTED.

ANSWERS ON PAGE 124

DISCUSS

1. What do you think of people who spend all of their money on designer labels? Tell why you think so.
   a. They are fashionable.
   b. They are foolish.
2. Where would you prefer to buy a pair of jeans? Tell why.
   a. the shijang (10,000 won)
   b. a discount store (15,000 won)
   c. a department store (100,000 won)
3. If you were very <u>rich</u>, where <u>would</u> you buy your jeans? Why?
   a. the shijang
   b. a discount store
   c. a department store
4. When you see people wearing expensive clothes, do you want to own the same things? Why or why not?
5. Why do many Koreans want to own expensive cars and designer clothes? Tell why you think so.
   a. ...to impress other people
   b. ...to feel successful in life
   c. ...because they were poor when they were young
6. What do you think is the best way to use your money? Tell why.
   a. Spend it. b. Save it. c. Give it to the poor
7. Do you buy clothes very often? If so, how often and where do you shop?
8. Do you enjoy spending money? Why or why not?

UNIT 33

CARS AND DRIVING

SAFE DRIVING

In Korea it is not common for teenagers to have drivers' licenses, but in some countries like the USA and New Zealand people get their licenses when they are still in high school. In these countries 14 or 15 years old is old enough to drive a car.

High schools offer driver's education courses, and all students, both girls and boys, take the course. In the course students learn how to drive a car, but they also learn how to drive safely.

Being a good driver involves more than just learning how to operate the controls. It also means being considerate of other drivers and sometimes giving up the right of way.

It means driving at safe speeds and obeying traffic laws.

UNSAFE DRIVING. THIS DRIVER DIDN'T OBEY TRAFFIC LAWS.

HARD WORDS

- **take...course**: study and take tests
- **operate...controls**: use the pedals and buttons
- **considerate**: kind and thoughtful
- **giving...way**: letting other drivers go first
- **safe speeds**: not too fast

USING A CELL PHONE WHILE DRIVING IS NOT A SAFE WAY TO DRIVE.

Unsafe driving Cell phones have added a new danger to driving that didn't exist before.

So many accidents have been caused by people talking or texting on cell phones while driving. Drivers on cell phones concentrate on their conversations and not on their driving.

As a result, they sometimes run through red lights or fail to stop at stop signs, even though they would never do those things intentionally.

Loud music Something that young drivers sometimes do is to play their CDs or MP3 players too loud. The music is a distraction and makes them forget about their driving. The music also bothers other drivers.

Another thing that drivers should never do is eat while they drive. Sometimes accidents are caused by people who are eating or drinking while driving their cars.

HARD WORDS

- **texting**: typing a message to someone on a call phone
- **concentrate (on)**: to think about
- **run...lights**: not stop for a red light
- **do intentionally**: do it on purpose
- **distraction**: make somebody think about it instead of their driving

THIS ISN'T A REAL CRASH. POLICE PUT IT THERE TO STOP UNSAFE DRIVING. DO YOU THINK IT WILL WORK?

PRACTICE

MAKE NEW SENTENCES USING THE WORDS IN GREEN.

...to give up... 1. She...drinking coffee 2. I...eating fatty fast food 3. He...drinking and driving	MY FATHER GAVE UP SMOKING 3 YEARS AGO. 
...to concentrate (on) 4. He…they are singing. 5. I...dogs are barking 6. He...loud music is playing	 DRIVERS CAN'T CONCENTRATE WHILE USING CELL PHONES.

DISCUSS

ANSWERS ON PAGE 124

1. Do you have a driver's license? If not, would you like to have one? If so, why?
2. What is the minimum age for a driver's license in Korea? Do you agree with that age or should it be lower? If so, why?
3. Korean roads are crowded. Do you agree with any of these suggestions for reducing the number of cars on the road? Why or why not?
   a. Raise the minimum age for a driver's license to 21.
   b. Make the driving test for a license much harder than it is now.
   c. Limit the number of drivers licenses to just 2 per family.
4. Do most Korean drivers obey traffic laws? Tell why you think so.
   a. Yes, most of them always obey traffic laws.
   b. No, they don't. Too many drivers ignore the traffic laws.
5. Should drivers be arrested if they use a cell phone while driving? If not, should they be punished at all? If so, how?
6. What kind of punishment should be given to drivers who drink alcohol (beer, whiskey) and drive and then cause accidents?
7. What do you think of women drivers? Are they worse, the same as, or better than men drivers? Tell why you think so.
8. Car insurance is less expensive for older drivers than for young drivers. Why is it more expensive for younger drivers?

9. What kind of punishment should drivers who do these things receive? Fine? Jail time? If so, how much?
   a. Run (ignore) red lights
   b. Don't stop at stop signs
   c. Drink alcohol and drive
   d. Talk on cell phones

UNIT 34 UFOs AND CIRCLES

THE UFO MYSTERY

Everybody knows that UFO stands for **U**nidentified **F**lying **O**bject, but are they real? If so, where are they from and what do they want? And why are they here?

There are a few theories about UFOs. Some people think they are spaceships with aliens inside. Other people are skeptics who think that people who report seeing UFOs or aliens are either lying or crazy.

But the number of people who believe that UFOs are real is increasing because too many UFO reports cannot be explained away. Amazing photos of UFOs seen all around the world have been analyzed.

Some of those sightings have occurred in Korea, and many have even been captured on film.

Seokcho City Hall, 2003

On September 17, 2003 an amazing UFO was seen by hundreds of people over Seokcho City Hall. It started out as 6 lights, but then separated into 10 lights (photo). The lights then joined together again and disappeared in a flash. No airplane or helicopter could do those things, and no human could survive that kind of speed. The event was captured on film by Yonhap News and shown on TV.

HARD WORDS

- **skeptics**: non-believers
- **to explain away**: say that it is an airplane or something ordinary
- **analyzed**: be studied very closely
- **to capture...firm**: take a movie of it
- **to survive**: to live, not die

CROP CIRCLES

Is it possible that aliens are leaving signs on the earth for us to see? The signs are called crop circles, and they are very beautiful and very complex. They are made in fields of grain, such as wheat or barley.

We know that some of the circles are made by humans, but others are too huge, too complex, and too perfect. Sometimes they appear in just a few minutes. Humans don't have the technology to do that.

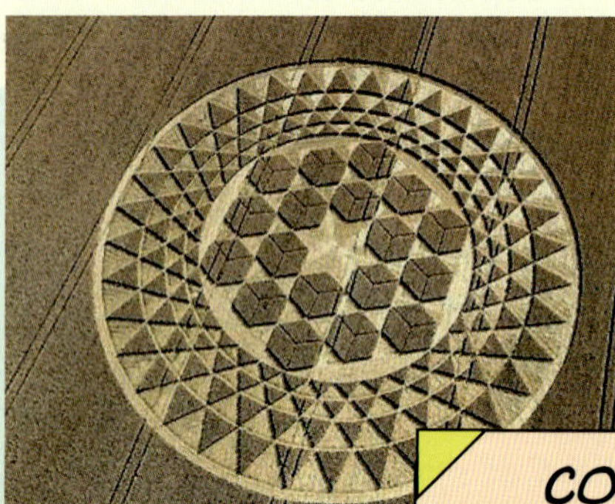

Lewisham Castle, Wiltshire Aug. 6, 2004

In the crop circle above, there are 13 kinds of symbols, each representing a number. All of the rows and columns (the horizontals and verticals) and diagonals add up to 369.

37	78	29	70	21	62	13	54	5
6	38	79	30	71	22	63	14	46
47	7	39	80	31	72	23	55	15
16	48	8	40	81	32	64	24	56
57	17	49	9	41	73	33	65	25
26	58	18	50	1	42	74	34	66
67	27	59	10	51	2	43	75	35
36	68	19	60	11	52	3	44	76
77	28	69	20	61	12	53	4	45

The symbols are arranged like the colors in this chart. Each color means a different symbol. All of the purples add up to 369. Is any human smart enough to design this chart? If so, would a person so smart be outside in fields making crop circles?

COULD HUMANS MAKE THIS IN JUST MINUTES?

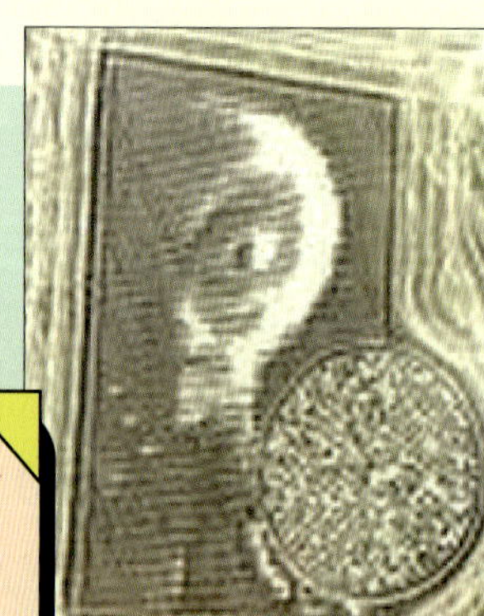

2001 CROP CIRCLE. IS THIS WHAT THEY LOOK LIKE?

HARD WORDS

- **complex**: very difficult, not simple
- **too perfect**: men couldn't do it
- **horizontals...**: lines that go from side to side or up and down

  V
  H

- **diagonals**: lines that go from one corner to another corner

PRACTICE

FILL IN THE MISSING WORD.

1. People who don't believe in UFOs are______.
2. Some UFO sightings can't be______ ______.
3. No human could_______ flying that fast.
4. Mankind doesn't have the_____ to do it.
5. Even the _______ add up to 369.
6. That crop circle has 13 kinds of ______.
7. Many UFOs have been _______ on film.
8. Crop circles are made in ______ of grain.

A. DIAGONALS
B. SURVIVE
C. CAPTURED
D. SYMBOLS
E. SKEPTICS
F. EXPLAINED AWAY
G. FIELDS
H. TECHNOLOGY
I. COMPLEX

ANSWERS ON PAGE 125

DISCUSS

1. What do you think UFOs are? Tell why you think so.
   a. They are aliens flying around the earth.
   b. They are people flying around in airplanes and helicopters.
   c. They are car lights or some other lights from the earth.
2. Have you ever seen a UFO? If so, tell about it. If not, would you like to see a UFO? Why or why not?
3. What would most people do if they saw a real alien? Tell why you think so.
   a. They would try to meet him.
   b. They would run away in fear.
   c. They would try to kill it.

ALL LINES ADD UP TO 369

4. Is any person smart enough to design this crop circle? If so, how long would it take, and would a person who is that smart be outside at night making crop circles, sometimes in the rain?
5. Why would anybody lie about seeing a UFO if they didn't really see one? Do you think these people are lying or crazy?
6. If the crop circles are made by aliens, why are they making them? Are the aliens trying to tell us something? If so, what?
7. Some of the circles are made by humans. Why do they make them?
8. If UFOs and crop circles are real, why are aliens here? What do they want? Are they friendly or not? Tell why you think so.
9. If UFOs and crop circles are real, why don't the aliens talk to us instead of just leaving signs?
10. In almost every movie that shows aliens, the aliens are "bad guys" trying to kill humans. Do you think that's a good way to show aliens? Why or why not?

UNIT 35 DINOSAURS

WHEN DINOSAURS WALKED THE EARTH

Three of the most popular movies of the 1990s were Jurassic Park and the two sequels that followed it. All three movies were box-office hits.

Why are movies about dinosaurs so popular? Because people young and old in every country around the world are fascinated by dinosaurs. It's because dinosaurs were enormous and because they ruled the earth for 150 million years.

Dinosaurs were the largest animals that ever walked the earth. One of them, the brachiosaurus, was 10 meters high, 25 meters long, and weighed 40 tons. But paleontologists are still learning about dinosaurs. A dinosaur discovered in 1985 was 54 meters long and lived 225 million years ago. It was named "Supersaurus" because it was the biggest dinosaur that ever lived.

SUPERSAURUS WAS 54 METERS LONG

HARD WORDS

- **sequels**: movies that continue the same story
- **(be) fascinated**: very interested in
- **enormous**: extremely big, huge
- **paleontologists**...study dino bones

Before 1817 nobody knew that dinosaurs had ever existed. In that year an English scientist named William Buckland found the tooth of a huge animal. Scientists were shocked. They didn't know that such a large animal had ever lived on the earth.

By 1850 huge teeth and huge bones were also found, and the name *dinosaur* was born.

We now know that they were the largest land animals that ever lived on the earth, and we know when they lived. They ruled the earth much longer than man has. This chart shows the comparison between the 150,000,000 years that the dinosaurs lived and the 100,000 years that man has lived.

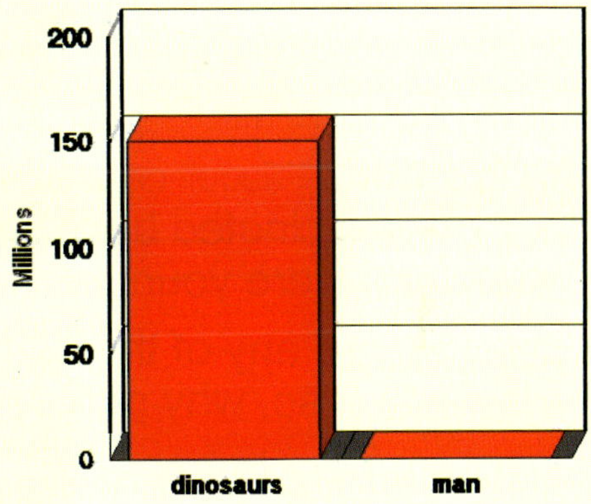

In comparison, man has only just arrived on the earth.

Even though huge dinosaurs like the ones in Jurassic Park aren't alive anymore, their descendants still are—birds. Birds are today's little dinosaurs.

THEN AND NOW

HARD WORDS

- **knew...existed**: know that there used to be dinosaurs on the earth
- **ruled...earth**: they were the strongest animals on the earth
- **only...arrived**: arrived here just a short time ago
- **descendants**: their children, and their children's children and so on

PRACTICE

FILL IN THE CORRECT WORD.

1. People are_______ by dinosaurs.
2. Jurassic Park was a box office _____.
3. Dinosaurs _____the world for 150 million years.
4. _____ dig up and study dinosaur bones.
5. Nobody knew that dinosaurs_______.
6. Dinosaurs were the biggest ______animals.
7. Scientists were ______when they saw that huge bone.
8. Birds are the ______ of dinosaurs.

A. PALEONTOLOGISTS
B. LAND
C. DESCENDANTS
D. RULED
E. EXISTED
F. FASCINATED
G. SHOCKED
H. HIT

ANSWERS ON PAGE 125

DISCUSS

1. Are you fascinated by dinosaurs? Were you fascinated by dinosaurs when you were younger?
2. Did you see any of the Jurassic Park movies? Did you like those movies? If so, why did you like them?

3. Why are people interested in dinosaurs, even though there are no real dinosaurs in the world? Tell why you think so.
4. If it were possible to bring dinosaurs back to life, would that be a good idea? Tell why you think so.
   a. Yes, bring them back to life.
   b. Bring back the plant-eaters, but not the meat-eaters.
   c. No, don't bring ANY dinosaurs back to life.
5. If dinosaurs lived on the earth today, would we be able to control them. Tell why you think so.
   a. Yes, we could control them.
   b. Just the little ones.
   c. Never. They would eat us.
6. If Jurassic Park were real, would you go there to see the dinosaurs? Why or why not?

7. If dinosaurs lived today, where would they live? Would it be possible to make them stay in the same place ? Why or why not?
8. Some people think that all animals should live in the wild, not in zoos. What do you think about that? Tell why you think so.
9. Dinosaurs lived on earth for 150,000,000 years. Will man rule the earth for that long too?

UNIT 36 ANIMALS AND PETS

A CUTE PUPPY

DOGS AS PETS

More and more Koreans are adopting pets these days. More people keep dogs as pets than any other kind of animal. We can tell because Korean supermarkets and discount stores carry a bigger supply of food and toys for dogs than for any other kind of animal.

Dogs can be great house pets because they are lovable and loyal to their owners. They also have sharp teeth and a loud bark, so they can scare away thieves. But they can also scare away friends, because many people are afraid of dogs.

We sometimes see dogs tied up outside, never allowed to run free. Their owners keep them only to protect their house from thieves. But dogs need a lot of exercise. Keeping a dog tied up all the time is a horrible life for a dog.

DOGS COME IN ALL SIZES

HARD WORDS

- **We...tell**: same as "we can see..." or "we can know..."
- **carry**: sell
- **house pet**: any animal that lives inside the house with people
- **loyal**: love and obey (their owners)

DOGS VS. CATS

But dogs aren't the only animals that make good pets. Cats can make excellent companions, and so can birds. These animals also can be loveable, and they are usually quieter than dogs.

Cats are very clean animals. They clean themselves with their tongues almost continuously. Because they are clean, their fur smells sweet. Dogs don't clean themselves, so they have to be given baths. If dogs don't get a bath, they stink.

Cats don't have to be taken outside for walks; dogs do. Dogs have to be taken out 2 or 3 times a day. Cats will use their own toilets (called litter boxes) inside the house. Dogs don't know how to do that.

Birds also make good house pets. They are much smarter than most people think, and some of them can even learn to talk. But pet birds must have their wings clipped. If not, someday they will fly away through an open window or door.

TEACHING A BIRD TO WHISTLE

HARD WORDS

- **companion**: living partner, close friend
- **fur**: an animal's hair
- **stink**: smell bad, have a bad odor
- **have...clipped**: cut off the ends of their feathers so that they can't fly

PRACTICE

MAKE NEW SENTENCES USING THE WORDS IN GREEN.

...to tell 1. My mother...wash my face 2. The teacher...do my homework 3. She...had gotten a haircut	I COULD **TELL** THAT YOU DIDN'T STUDY FOR THAT TEST. 
...to keep...continuously 4. She...watching TV... 5. The baby...crying... 6. The children...fighting...	 THE DOGS **KEPT** BARKING **CONTINUOUSLY**.

ANSWERS ON PAGE 125

DISCUSS

AUTHOR JACK MARTIRE AND PET LOVEBIRD "BEEP"

1. Do you have a pet? If so, what kind of animal is it and when did you get it?
2. Should everybody have a pet? Why or why not?
3. What kind of animal do you think makes the best pet? Tell why you think so.
4. Do fish make good pets? Why or why not?
5. Some people like to keep dangerous animals—snakes, lions, sharks, etc.—as pets. Which of these statements do you agree with and why?
   a. Dangerous animals should never be kept as pets.
   b. It's okay to have dangerous animals if they are not wild.
   c. Baby dangerous animals are okay, but not big ones.
6. Are people who have pets different from people who don't like animals? If so, how are they different?
7. Some people treat their pets like babies. They buy them clothes and dye their fur different colors. What do you think of that? Would you do that? Why or why not?
8. Old people who have pets live longer than old people who do not have pets. Why do you think that is so?
9. Dogs are very smart animals, but some Koreans like to eat them. Do you think it's okay to eat smart animals? Why or why not?
   a. It's okay to eat dumb animals but not smart ones.
   b. It's okay to eat any animal. Animals were made to be eaten.
   c. People shouldn't eat animals at all. (Why not?)
10. Some people don't eat any meat. They are called vegetarians. Can a person be healthy eating just vegetables?

UNIT 37 PROFESSIONAL SPORTS

Professional sports are very popular in Korea. There are soccer teams, baseball teams, and basketball teams. Cities all over the country have teams. Most people root for their hometown teams.

The game of baseball was invented in North America in the early 1800s, and the first US teams were organized in the 1850s. Baseball is called America's "national pastime".

The only countries outside North America where there are professional baseball teams are Japan and South Korea. American missionaries brought the game to Korea in 1904.

The first baseball team in Korea was a high school team. It was formed in 1905. Korea's pro baseball league was organized in 1982, and now there are 8 teams.

KOREAN PRO BASEBALL TEAM LOGOS

HARD WORDS

- **to root (for)**: to cheer for
- **to organize**: to form into a team of players
- **pastime**: enjoyable activity, do it for fun
- **missionaries**: workers for Christian churches

Just as in the USA, Korean baseball fans love their teams and get very excited at baseball games. Korean teams even have their own cheerleaders.

Baseball is a kind of team sport. That means that several players play together as a team. Other team sports include soccer, volleyball, basketball, and hockey, just to name a few.

In baseball, as in all team sports, whether a team wins or loses depends on two main factors: 1) how well each individual player plays, and 2) how well all the players play together as a group.

Players who play exceptionally well usually become famous. Sometimes a Korean player joins a baseball team in the US. Such players always become stars both in Korea and in the USA.

It is the dream of every professional team player to become a superstar.

HOW MANY OF THESE TEAM SPORTS CAN YOU NAME?

HARD WORDS

- **team sport**: players work together, not alone
- **just...few**: there are more than just these
- **play...well**: are very good players, better than normal
- **superstar**: also "megastar", famous in the world

ANSWERS

a.basketball
b.football
c.soccer
d.hockey
e.water polo
f. rugby

PRACTICE

FILL IN THE CORRECT WORD.

1. Most people_______ for their teams.
2. Baseball was _____in the 1800s.
3. Sports are a _____for many people.
4. Korea's baseball _____was formed in 1982.
5. Soccer is a kind of _____sport.
6. She plays golf_____ well.
7. Every player wants to become a_____.
8. It is the ____of every player.

A. EXCEPTIONALLY
B. INVENTED
C. DREAM
D. PASTIME
E. TEAM
F. ROOT
G. SUPERSTAR
H. ORGANIZED
I. LEAGUE

DISCUSS

ANSWERS ON PAGE 125

1. Do you have a favorite sport? If so, what is it, and do you play or just watch?
2. Are you a fan of pro baseball? If so, what's your favorite team?
3. Have you ever gone to a professional baseball game? Which is better—watching a game on TV or watching the game at the stadium?
4. Famous sports stars in some countries receive huge salaries. What do you think of that? Tell why you think so.
   a. Players should not receive huge salaries.
   b. It doesn't matter. The more money, the better.
5. Do you prefer watching team sports or individual sports competitions? Tell why you think so.
6. What is the most important reason why athletes want to play on professional teams? Tell why you think so.
   a. ...because they love to play the sport.
   b. ...so that they can become famous.
   c. ...so that they can make a lot of money.

FOOTBALL

7. Which type of sport do you think is more exciting to watch—the Olympic competitions or professional sports? Tell why you think so.
8. Would you like to play for a professional sports team? Why or why not?
9. How important are professional sports in our lives? Why are sports competitions important? Why or why not?
10. How can sports play an important role in improving relations between countries that don't like each other?

UNIT 38

HOBBIES

TIME TO RELAX

Most Korean high school students don't have much free time, especially if they're planning to go to college. Getting ready for college in Korea means spending long hours studying for college entrance tests. It also means learning English.

But everyone, even a high school student, needs some time to relax his or her mind. Everyone, young or old, should have at least one hobby or interest to take his or her mind off work or study sometimes.

SPORTS For many teenage boys playing some kind of sport is a hobby. Anything from playing soccer with friends to bodybuilding in the gym to flying a kite are good ways to take a rest from schoolwork and studying for college entrance exams.

HARD WORDS

- **free time**: time when not working or studying
- **relax...mind**: to rest, not worry about anything
- **take...off**: think about something other than work or study
- **to fly a kite**: This is a kite.

COMPUTERS For many boys, and some girls too, using a computer and connecting to the Internet is a pastime. It is also a great way to learn. But since the Internet is also fun, it is easy to spend too much time online while neglecting schoolwork.

MUSIC Listening to music, particular pop music, is a favorite pastime for girls and boys. Most of them enjoy collecting CDs of their favorite singers. One drawback to this hobby is that CDs are expensive. But now we can download MP3 songs from the Internet.

ART Teenagers who are talented in art spend their time drawing or painting. For these kids, art is more than just a pastime. Many of them are preparing for future careers in design or architecture.

So there are many kinds of hobbies that teenagers can have. Besides being a way to relax the mind, a hobby can also be a good way to prepare for a future job or career.

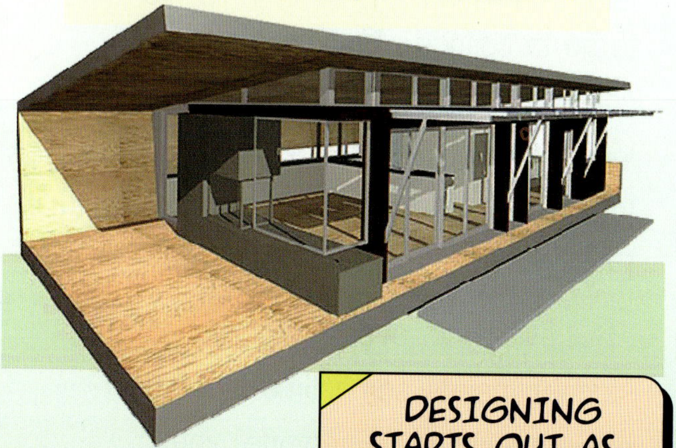

DESIGNING STARTS OUT AS LIKING TO DRAW

PAINTING STARTS OUT AS A HOBBY

BECOMING A COMPUTER EXPERT BEGINS AS A HOBBY

HARD WORDS

- **to neglect**: to ignore, not do it, forget about it
- **drawback**: disadvantage, something bad about it
- **(be) talented**: have a special ability to do it well
- **architecture**: designing buildings

PRACTICE

FILL IN THE CORRECT WORD.

1. You should take your mind ____ your studies sometimes.
2. Korean students don't have much free_____.
3. Everyone needs a _____ to rest his or her mind.
4. A hobby can help prepare for a future _____.
5. Students don't have a lot of money to_____.
6. Don't spend too much time _____.
7. Don't _____ your studies.
8. He is very _____ in music.

A. HOBBY
B. NEGLECT
C. ONLINE
D. PASTIME
E. CAREER
F. OFF
G. SPEND
H. TALENTED
I. TIME

ANSWERS ON PAGE 125

DISCUSS

1. What is your hobby or special interest? When did you first become interested in that and how often do you do it?
2. Which of these statements do you agree with and why?
   a. Yes, every teenager should have a hobby to take their minds off studying sometimes.
   b. No, students should not take time off from studying. They have to study hard, so there is no time for hobbies.
3. How much time should be spent on hobbies or special interests outside of school? Tell why you think so.
   a. A little time every day.
   b. Just on the weekends.
   c. No time for hobbies until after the college entrance test
4. Korean students spend most of their time studying and going to hagwons from when they are little kids. Should more time be spent on hobbies and less on studying? Why or why not?
5. Which of these activities are good hobbies for high school students and which are not? Tell why you think so.
   a. playing the piano
   b. computer gaming
   c. drawing pictures
   d. playing soccer
   e. bodybuilding
   f. watching TV
   g. hiking
   h. Internet chat rooms
   i. learning English
6. Is it possible for a person to study too much and not get enough rest? Why or why not?
7. Should every high school student belong to a school club or a sports team? Why or why not?
8. Should a part of the school day be used for activities not related to studying or taking tests? Why or why not?

UNIT 39 COMPUTER GAMING

A GAMER'S WORLD

Korea is the world capital of computer gaming. Internet gamers from all over the world come to Korea to compete in gaming competitions.

There are thousands of game rooms spread all over the country, and most of them are open 24 hours a day. That's because when gamers start playing a game, they can't just stop playing and go home. They play with gamers all over the world, so when it's late at night in Korea it might be the middle of the day someplace else.

LINEAGE -- A FAMOUS KOREAN COMPUTER GAME

The reason that Korea became a gamer's paradise is because Korea was quick to become wired with broadband. Gaming requires lightning-fast Internet connections, and Korea was one of the first countries to have them.

HARD WORDS

- **gamers**: people play computer games
- **compete**: to play against other players to win
- **wired**: have fast connections to the Internet
- **broadband**: a very fast Internet connection

AN AVATAR

The world of a computer game is surreal because of the CGI graphics used to make them. Players become involved in the action because of the amazing locations and because the action seems to be really happening. Each player chooses an *avatar* to represent himself in the game.

Most teenagers, especially boys, are interested in computer gaming, but parents and teachers are not. They see it as a waste of time .

A study that was conducted by a university in Canada in 2003 found that students who play Internet games have better visual acuity and react faster in emergencies than students who don't play the games.

But most Korean parents still think that kids should spend their time studying for their exams and not playing computer games.

But an even bigger problem is computer game addiction. Some students become so interested in the games that they can't pull themselves away.

"You wanted wireless video gaming? You got it. Now, go outside and play."

ADDICTED TO GAMING

HARD WORDS

- **(be) surreal**: even better and more amazing than real life
- **to see...as**: ...think that it is...
- **visual acuity**: can notice very small details very easily
- **react...emergencies**: think faster in an emergency, like a car accident
- **addiction**: can't stop, want to do it all the time
- **pull...away**: can't stop doing it because they are having so much fun

PRACTICE

FILL IN THE CORRECT WORD.

1. Korea is the world's gaming _____.
2. Gaming isn't possible without _____ connections.
3. Korea was one of the first _____ countries in the world.
4. CGI stands for computer generated _____.
5. Every gamer has his or her own _____.
6. Most parents think that gaming is a ____ of time.
7. In fact, gamers have better visual _____.
8. Gamers who can't stop playing are _____ to gaming.

A. WIRED
B. ACUITY
C. CAPITAL
D. IMAGING
E. AVATAR
F. ADDICTED
G. BROADBAND
H. IMAGERY
I. WASTE

ANSWERS ON PAGE 125

DISCUSS

1. Are you a gamer? Do you like playing computer games? If so, what do you like about it? If not, why don't you like computer games?
2. What do you think about Korea being the gaming capital of the world? Tell why you think so.
   a. I think it's great. It's a big honor for the country.
   b. It's not important. Gaming is nothing to be proud of.
3. Do Koreans like gaming more than people in other countries? Why did gaming become so popular in Korea?
4. Generally speaking, Asians like gaming more than people in western countries. Why do you think that is so?
5. Boys usually like gaming more than girls do. Why don't girls and women like gaming as much? Tell why you think so.
6. In the USA, the average age of gamers is 33, but the average game buyer is 40. How can you explain the age difference?
7. In the U.K., the average age of gamers is just 23, but it is 33 in the US. What do you guess is the average age of gamers in Korea? Tell why you think so.
8. What do you think of Korean game rooms? Are they good places for young people to hang out? Why or why not?
9. Some people become addicted to gaming, but others don't. Why do some people get addicted while others know when it is time to quit? Tell why you think so.
10. What is the best thing to do with a student who doesn't want to do anything except play video games? Tell why you think so.

UNIT 40

RELIGION

TOP 10 BUDDHIST COUNTRIES

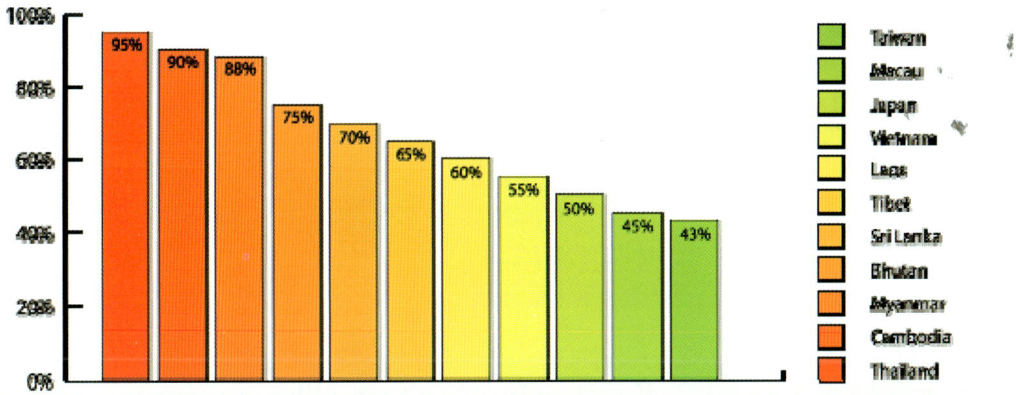

KOREAN CHRISTIANITY

There are many places to pray in Korea. Besides the many Buddhist temples, there are also hundreds of Christian churches.

But Korea is the only Asian country where Christianity is popular. In all other Asian countries Christian churches are hard to find.

Why, then, are there so many Christians in Korea? What makes Korea special? It is because of the 35-years between 1910 and 1945 when Japan occupied Korea. During that period Christianity became Korea's way to fight against the Japanese.

The first Christian churches in Korea were built by Catholic missionaries in the late 1800s, but it wasn't until after the Japanese invaded Korea in 1910 that Christianity caught on.

Korea's Japanese rulers didn't permit the Korean language to be used, but Christian groups kept it alive by printing church teachings in hangul.

HARD WORDS

- **(be) hard...find**: are very rare
- **occupied**: sent in their army
- **invaded**: same as "occupied"
- **to catch on**: become popular
- **to keep...alive**: make people not forget about it

A KOREAN CHRISTIAN WEDDING

So while Christians were keeping the Korean language alive during that Japanese occupation, it was also a good way for them to spread their religious beliefs to the Korean people.

Today there are many different Christian sects in Korea, including Catholics, Baptists, Methodists, Presbyterians, and Mormons. These are all different groups of Christians.

The customs differ from one sect to another, but all of them share a belief in Jesus Christ, who they believe lived 2,000 years ago, as the savior of mankind.

But Christianity is something very new in Korea's history. Korea's roots are in Buddhism, the same as all other Asian countries. There are still more Buddhist temples than Christian churches in Korea.

Christianity goes back less than 150 years in Korea, but Buddhism can be traced all the way back to 372 A.D., when it was introduced from China.

The most interesting thing about religion in Korea is that even though there are lots of Buddhist temples and Christian churches here, most Koreans say that they have no religion.

A FAMOUS OLD KOREAN BUDDHIST TEMPLE

HARD WORDS

- **sect**: a different division or group
- **to share...belief**: They all agree.
- **savior...mankind**: "save" mankind from burning in hell *(that's what they believe)*
- **roots**: history, how long it has been a part of Korea
- **(be) traced**: how many years ago it began

PRACTICE

FILL IN THE CORRECT WORD

1. Christianity is not very_____ in most Asian countries.
2. Christian churches are hard to _____ in Asia.
3. Buddhism was _____ to Korea from China in 372 A.D.
4. The Japanese army _____ Korea in 1910.
5. Christianity didn't _____on in Korea until after 1910.
6. Missionaries_____ their beliefs to the Korean people.
7. There are many different_____ of Christianity.
8. Buddhism can be_____ back further than Christianity.

A. SPREAD
B. INTRODUCED
C. INVADED
D. SECTS
E. CATCH
F. FIND
G. TRACED
H. POPULAR
I. SECTIONS

ANSWERS ON PAGE 125

DISCUSS

1. Are you a member of a religion? If so, what is your religion and how did you become a member?
2. What do you think is the main reason why people join Christian churches? Tell why you think so.
   a. ...because they love God
   b. ...because the churches are like social clubs with parties
   c. ...because they want God to help them with their problems
3. Should every adult be a member of a church or religion? Why or why not?
4. Are children who go to church better students than children who do not go to church? Tell why you think so.
5. Are people who go to church more honest or kinder than people who do not go to church? Tell why you think so.
6. Are Christians more religious than Buddhists or are both groups just the same? Tell why you think so.
7. Most Koreans say that they do not belong to any religion. Why are they less religious than people in Southeast Asia where 95% are Buddhists?
8. Is there a God? If so, does God like religious people more than people who are not religious? Tell why you think so.
9. Does a person have to go to church in order to go to heaven after he or she dies, or doesn't it matter? Tell why you think so.
10. What do you think happens to people after they die? Tell why you think so.
    a. They all go to heaven or hell. b. Nothing happens, it's just black.

BUDDHIST MONKS IN THAILAND

ANSWERS TO PRACTICE QUESTIONS

UNIT 1 (PAGE 4)
1. She keeps all her personal belongings in her closet.
2. I keep all my personal belongings in my book bag.
3. You keep all your personal belongings in your room.
4. We socialize on weekends.
5. My sister socializes at church.
6. He socializes at club meetings.

UNIT 2 (PAGE 7)
1. She envies him for being so smart.
2. They envy him for being so rich.
3. He envies him for being so handsome.
4. The amount of love they get from their mother is equal.
5. The amount of enjoyment they get from singing is equal.
6. The amount of money they get from their father is equal.

UNIT 3 (PAGE 10)
1. I prepared for the party all week.
2. We prepared for the trip for a month.
3. They prepared for the meeting all day.
4. She resembles her mother.
5. I resemble my father.
6. My sister resembles our Aunt Susan.

UNIT 4 (PAGE 13)
1. There seems to be no end to the trouble that he makes.
2. There seems to be no end to the money that she spends.
3. There seems to be no end to the things that I lose.
4. Whether you get the job depends on how well you can speak English.
5. Whether your sister gets the job depends on how well she can read.
6. Whether he gets the job depends on how well he can drive a car.

UNIT 5 (PAGE 16)
1. Children should obey their parents.
2. Dogs should obey their masters.
3. Drivers should obey traffic laws.
4. He was arrested for robbing a store.
5. They were arrested for stealing a car.
6. The boys were arrested for fighting.

UNIT 6 (PAGE 19)
1. pregnancy
2. sexually
3. babies
4. class
5. romantic
6. puberty
7. reality
8. less

UNIT 7 (PAGE 22)
1. He doesn't stand a chance of getting that job.
2. She doesn't stand a chance of dating that guy.
3. I don't stand a chance of getting an A in math.
4. I want to put an end to her phone calls.
5. He wants to put an end to his dog's barking.
6. She wants to put an end to the baby's crying

UNIT 8 (PAGE 25)
1. How long did it take for your sister to get to school?
2. How long did it take for your father to get to work by bus?
3. How long did it take for you to get to Cheju by boat?
4. My father was swamped with office work.
5. I was swamped with book reports and tests.
6. The hospital was swamped with new patients.

UNIT 9 (PAGE 28)
1. He tried to get into school but failed.
2. I wanted to get into the club but gave up.
3. I tried to get into the meeting but couldn't.
4. You can decide whether to stay here or (to) go home.
5. They can decide whether to do homework or (to) play.
6. He can decide whether to play tennis or soccer.

UNIT 10 (PAGE 31)
1. Long hair caught on in the mid-1960s.
2. The Internet caught on in the late 1990s.
3. Studying abroad caught on in 1996.
4. He could never get used to eating Indian food.
5. They could never get used to traveling by plane.
6. I could never get used to Seoul's cold winters.

UNIT 11 (PAGE 34)
1. She's just 5 years old, but already she has ideas of her own.
2. They're just 5 years old, but already they have ideas of their own.
3. My brother is just 5 years old, but already he has ideas of his own.
4. My boyfriend tries hard to impress his teachers.
5. You try hard to impress your teachers.
6. Our friends try hard to impress their teachers.

ANSWERS TO PRACTICE QUESTIONS

UNIT 12 (PAGE 37)
1. center
2. turns into
3. relationships
4. rejected
5. break
6. schedules
7. independent
8. pressures

UNIT 13 (PAGE 40)
1. She hangs out with the same friends that she grew up with.
2. They hang out with the same friends that they grew up with.
3. My brother hangs out with the same friends that he grew up with.
4. He can't relate to the life of his teenage son.
5. She can't relate to the lives of her teenage kids.
6. They can't relate to the life of their teenage daughter.

UNIT 14 (PAGE 43)
1. The birthday party lasted 2 hours.
2. The rain lasted just 10 minutes.
3. A cell phone lasts a few years.
4. She spends 10,000 won a week.
5. I spent 5,000 won yesterday.
6. We spent 5 hours studying last night.

UNIT 15 (PAGE 46)
1. Stores are (always) jammed with people (or shoppers) on Sunday.
2. Subways are (sometimes) jammed with people
3. The beach is jammed with swimmers (or people) in summer.
4. Most men wouldn't want to be seen in a dress shop.
5. Most women wouldn't want to be seen without (their) makeup.
6. Most teachers wouldn't want to be seen at a nightclub.

UNIT 16 (PAGE 49)
1. The amount of homework has recently been cut in half.
2. College tuition has recently been cut in half.
3. The number of students has recently been cut in half.
4. She wishes (that) she had a lot of money.
5. He wishes (that) he could buy a new car.
6. They wish (that) they could move to Cheju.

UNIT 17 (PAGE 52)
1. equivalent.
2. forced
3. injury.
4. obey.
5. safety
6. booster
7. complain.
8. trouble

UNIT 18 (PAGE 55)
1. You can go whenever you want.
2. You can visit whoever you want (*whomever* is grammatically correct, but people always say *whoever*)
3. You can eat whatever you want.
4. They don't have enough food to eat.
5. He doesn't have enough milk to drink.
6. You don't have enough money to spend. .

UNIT 19 (PAGE 58)
1. She had a hard time fitting into her new class.
2. He had a hard time fitting in at church.
3. They had a hard time fitting in at college.
4. Fathers have a lot of problems to deal with.
5. Students have a lot of tests to deal with.
6. Teachers have a lot of bad students to deal with.

UNIT 20 (PAGE 61)
1. She speaks two languages, so she is bi-lingual.
2. They speak many languages, so they are multilingual.
3. My mother speaks just Korean, so she is monolingual.
4. Dogs and cats are hard to spot in a crowd.
5. Bicycles are hard to spot on a busy street.
6. Small cars are hard to spot on the road.

UNIT 21 (PAGE 64)
1. The store ran out of milk last week.
2. We ran out of rice last week.
3. The printer ran out of paper last week.
4. I keep losing my cell phone.
5. The baby keeps losing its spoon.
6. He keeps losing his English book.

UNIT 22 (PAGE 67)
1. My homework piled up on my desk.
2. Snow piled up at the front door.
3. Their money piled up in the bank.
4. He used up all of the gas in his car.
5. Breakfast used up all of the eggs in the kitchen.
6. They used up all of the water in the can.

ANSWERS TO PRACTICE QUESTIONS

UNIT 23 (PAGE 70)

1. The Internet will be a lot faster this time next year.
2. Prices of LCD TVs will be a lot cheaper this time next year.
3. Gasoline will be a lot more expensive this time next year.

UNIT 24 (PAGE 73)

1. She arrived just in time to watch the TV program.
2. He arrived just in time to see the team win.
3. I arrived just in time to eat dinner with the family.
4. She can't imagine a time without cell phones.
5. He can't imagine a world without email.
6. We can't imagine a life without the Internet

UNIT 25 (PAGE 76)

1. She gave up swimming when she was 18.
2. He gave up playing baseball when he was 35.
3. He gave up stealing when he was arrested.
4. She couldn't handle her new English class.
5. He couldn't handle all of the homework.
6. We couldn't handle the long 12-hour drive.

UNIT 26 (PAGE 79)

1. TVs weren't sold in Korea until the 1970s.
2. Telephones weren't used by most people until the 1920s.
3. Our school wasn't built until 1999.

UNIT 27 (PAGE 82)

1. She got tired of watching the same TV show every-day.
2. He got tired of studying the same subject everyday.
3. They got tired of wearing the same uniforms every-day.
4. I wonder what kind of computers we'll be using 5 years from now.
5. I wonder what kind of cars we'll be driving 5 years from now.
6. I wonder what kind of TVs we'll be watching 5 years from now.

UNIT 28 (PAGE 85)

1. b
2. a
3. c
4. b
5. b
6. b

UNIT 29 (PAGE 88)

1. Her teaching skills are being wasted. They could be put to better use.
2. Too much food is being wasted. It could be put to better use.
3. The students' time is being wasted. It could be put to better use.
4. His tiny car is less than ideal for taking long trips.
5. Your clothes are less than ideal for cold weather.
6. My small house is less than ideal for big parties.

UNIT 30 (PAGE 91)

1. His new car was thanks to his getting a job.
2. Schools were closed thanks to the snow.
3. My bicycle was thanks to Santa Claus.
4. Eating ice cream for breakfast is out of the question.
5. Going hiking on a school day is out of the question.
6. Wearing shorts to class is out of the question.

UNIT 31 (PAGE 94)

1. Today's cell phones are more like computers than telephones.
2. Today's wide-screen TVs are more like movie screens than televisions.
3. Today's SUVs (Sports Utility Vehicles) are more like trucks than cars.
4. Eating ice cream for breakfast is out of the question.
5. Going hiking on a school day is out of the question.
6. Wearing shorts to class is out of the question.

UNIT 32 (PAGE 97)

1. She usually hangs out with her friends at the library.
2. They usually hang out with their friends on week-ends.
3. He usually hangs out with his friends at the gym.
4. She ended up with more trouble than she expected.
5. They ended up with more homework than they ex-pected.
6. My brother ended up with more problems than he expected.

UNIT 33 (PAGE 100)

1. She gave up drinking coffee 3 years ago.
2. I gave up eating fatty fast food 3 years ago.
3. He gave up drinking and driving 3 years ago.
4. He can't concentrate while they are singing.
5. I can't concentrate while dogs are barking.
6. He can't concentrate while loud music is playing.

ANSWERS TO PRACTICE QUESTIONS

UNIT 34 (PAGE 103)
1. skeptics
2. explained away
3. survive
4. technology
5. diagonals
6. symbols
7. captured
8. fields

UNIT 35 (PAGE 106)
1. fascinated
2. hit
3. ruled
4. paleontologists
5. existed
6. land
7. shocked
8. descendants

UNIT 36 (PAGE 109)
1. My mother could tell that I didn't wash my face.
2. The teach could tell that I didn't do my homework.
3. She could tell that I had gotten a haircut.
4. She kept watching TV continuously
5. The baby kept crying continuously.
6. The children kept fighting continuously.

UNIT 37 (PAGE 112)
1. root
2. invented
3. pastime
4. league
5. team
6. exceptionally
7. superstar
8. dream

UNIT 38 (PAGE 115)
1. off
2. time
3. hobby
4. career
5. spend
6. online
7. neglect
8. talented

UNIT 39 (PAGE 118)
1. capital
2. broadband
3. wired
4. imagery
5. avatar
6. waste
7. acuity
8. addicted

UNIT 40 (PAGE 121)
1. popular
2. find
3. introduced
4. invaded
5. catch
6. spread
7. sects
8. traced

INDEX OF WORDS AND PHRASES

1. HIGH SCHOOL LIFE

한국과 미국 고교 생활 비교

미국에서의 고교생활은 한국에서의 고교 생활과 매우 다르다. 물론, 어떤 것들은 같다 – 교실, 책, 선생님, 그리고 시험. 그러나 유사성은 거기서 끝난다.

등교 . 한가지 예로, 대부분의 한국 고교생들은 지하철이나 대중 버스를 이용하여 등교하지만, 미국 학생들의 대부분은 노란색 학교 버스를 타거나 차를 운전하여 등교한다. 대부분의 미국 고등학교는 학생들을 위한 주차장을 가지고 있다.

책과 학용품들. 한국 학생들은 책, 필기구, 그리고 다른 개인 소지품등을 무거운 가방에 가지고 학교에 다닌다. 그러나 미국 학생들은 책이나 다른 개인 소지품등을 학교 사물함 안에 보관한다. 그들은 단지 숙제하는데 필요한 책들만 집에 가져간다.

교복. 한국 학생들은 교복을 입으나 대부분 미국 학생들은 교복을 입지 않는다. 오직 사립학교에 다니는 소수의 학생들만 교복을 입는다.

파트타임 일하기. 대부분의 한국 고교생들에겐 파트타임으로 일하는 것이 상상할 수 없는 일이다. 그러나, 미국 십대들에겐 평범한 일이다. 그들은 패스트 푸드점, 세차장, 또는 슈퍼 등에서 파트타임으로 일한다. 미국인들은 부모로부터 돈을 쉽게 받는 십대들보다 스스로 용돈을 버는 십대들이 돈의 가치를 더 잘 안다고 생각한다.

사교생활. 미국 학생들은 학국의 학생들보다 파티나 소풍등의 자리에서 이성을 사귈 기회가 더 많이 있다. 미국 학생들은 남녀 모두 한반에서 공부를 하지만 한국은 각각 다른 교실에서 공부를 한다. 또한 미국 고교에서는 매주말마다 댄스파티가 열리지만 한국 고교에서는 그렇지 않다.

학교 교육과정. 한국과 미국 고교 모두 수학, 역사, 생물, 외국어, 아트 (미술) 그리고 음악 등의 다양한 정규 과목들을 가르친다. 하지만 한국 고교에서는 정규 과목으로 가르치지 않는 운전교육을 미국 고교에서는 정규 과목으로 가르친다. 미국은 아주 넓은 나라라서 운전은 살아가는데 필수이다. 그래서 미국에선 16세의 고교생들에게 운전교육은 필수이다.

교실. 한국 고교생들과 마찬가지로 미국 고교생들에게도 홈룸 (Homeroom – 조회, 종례 시간을 갖는 교실) 이 있다. 그러나, 미국 학생들은 하루 종일 같은 학생들과 수업을 받지 않는다. 같은 홈룸에 속한다 하더라도 학생들 모두 같은 과목을 같은 교실에서 공부하는 것은 아니다. 대학에서와 마찬가지로 각각의 과목마다 다른 교실에서 다른반 학생들과 수업을 받는다.

스포츠. 한국 고교에도 스포츠팀이 있지만, 미국 고교는 스포츠를 더 강조한다. 오른쪽에 전형적인 한 미국 고교의 다양한 스포츠 시간표가 있다.

컴퓨터 과목들. 거의 모든 미국의 고교에는 컴퓨터 교육 과정이 있다. 많은 학교에서는 학생들이 집에서 온라인 수업을 통해 공부할 수 있도록 하고 있다.

QUESTIONS FOR DISCUSSION

1. 여러분의 학교에 대해서 답하세요.
   a. 남녀공학, 아니면 남고 또는 여고?
   b. 이성이 같은 교실에서 수업하나요?
   c. 여러분 학년에 몇 개의 반이 있나요? 한 반에 학생수는?
   d. 하루 중에 가장 재미있는 학교 시간은? 이유는?
2. 미국의 여름방학은 3개월이다 그러나 겨울방학은 2주간이다. 한국에서는 언제가 여름과 겨울 방학인가요? 미국과 한국의 방학 시기중 어느쪽을 선호하나요? 이유는?
3. 고교생이 파트타임으로 일하는 것은 좋다고 생각하나요? 그 이유는? 만약 파트타임 일을 한다면 어떤 일을 하고 싶나요, 그리고 그 이유는?
4. 고교생이 차운전을 하는 것은 좋다고 생각하나요? 그 이유는? 몇살의 나이에 차운전을 배우는 것이 좋다고 생

각하나요? 왜 그렇게 생각하나요?

5. 학교에서 할 수 있는 스포츠 종목들은 무엇이 있나요? 여러분은 어떤 스포츠를 즐겨하나요?
6. 고교에서 열리는 댄스파티에 대해서 어떻게 생각하나요? 여러분의 학교에서도 댄스파티가 열리면 좋을까요?
7. 여러분의 학교는 컴퓨터 교육을 시키나요? 그렇다면, 컴퓨터 과목들이 필수인가요? 인터넷을 통해 들을 수 있는 과목도 있나요?
8. 여러분의 학교에는 특별활동반이 있나요? 어떤 반에 속해있나요? 얼마나 자주 모여서 무엇을 하나요?
9. 가장 선호하는 과목은? 왜 그 과목을 좋아하나요?

2. COEDUCATION

남녀공학과 동성(同姓) 학교/학급의 비교

한국의 초등학교는 남녀공학이지만 대부분의 중학교와 고등학교는 그렇지 않다. 한국에서 남녀 중고등학생들은 같은 학교에 다니는 것이 사실이지만 각각 동성으로만 이루어진 학급 (남학생반, 여학생반) 에서 공부를 한다. 한국의 학교는 남녀공학이지만 학급은 그렇지 않다고 말할 수 있다.

많은 한국의 중고등학생들은 대부분의 학교가 남녀공학인 미국이나 다른 서구 학교의 학생들을 부러워한다. 한국 학생들이 만약 이성의 학생들과 함께 공부한다면 더 잘 배울것이라고 생각한다. 그러나 대부분의 한국의 선생님들과 부모님들은 이에 동의하지 않는다.

교내에서 키스. 현재의 교육제도를 선호하는 한국 고교 선생님들은 남녀공학이 초래할 문제들을 피하고 싶다고 말한다. 이 문제들 중 하나는 십대의 로맨스이다. 만약 한국의 학생들이 미국, 영국, 또는 호주의 학교에 다닌다면 남녀 학생들이 교내에서 껴안거나, 심지어는 키스하는 것을 보고 아주 놀랄 것이다.

산만함. 이성과 한 교실에서 공부함으로써 학생들이 (학업에 집중못하고) 산만해지는 문제 때문에 미국의 몇몇 구역의 학교들은 현재 전체 남고 그리고 전체 여고를 시도해 보고 있다. 그 학교들은 학생들이 더 잘 배우기를 바란다. 남고와 여고로 분리된 학교의 선생님들은 그 학교의 학생들이 더 학업에 집중하고 열심히 배운다고 말한다.

불평등한 교육. 그러나 미국에선 남녀 학생을 분리하여 학교에 보낸다는 생각은 아주 급진적인 것이다. 그것은 전통을 벗어나는 것이다. 또한, 일부의 사람들은 만약 학생들이 남녀로 분리된 학교에 다닌다면 평등한 교육을 받지 못할 것이라고 우려한다.

남녀공학의 주된 목적은 여학생들이 남학생들과 동등한 교육을 받도록 하기 위함이다. 많은 나라들은 공립학교에서 남녀 학생들이 한 교실에서 함께 공부하도록 규정하는 법을 가지고 있다.

QUESTIONS FOR DISCUSSION

1. 한국의 남녀공학 학교에 대한 여러분의 견해는? 왜 그렇게 생각하나요.
   a. 남녀학생 모두 한 학급에서 공부해야 한다.
   b. 남녀학생들이 다른 학급에서 공부하는 것이 좋다고 생각한다.
2. 남녀학생들이 한 학급에서 공부하면 십대들이 더 사랑에 빠질 것이라고 생각하나요? 그 이유는?
3. 이성의 학생들이 한 학급에서 공부하면 학습에 집중하기 힘들다고 생각하나요?
   a. 집중하기 힘들다. b. 더 공부를 잘한다. c. 차이가 없다.
4. 여학생들만 한 학급에서 학습하면 남학생들과 동질의 교육을 받을 수 있나요? 아니면, 선생님들이 남학생들을

더 잘 가르치나요?

5. 남녀 학생들이 평등한 교육을 받아야 한다고 생각하나요, 아니면 남학생들이 더 나은 교육을 받아야 한다고 생각하나요? 왜 그렇게 생각하나요.
6. 왜 과거에 항상 한국 학교는 동성학교 교육제도였다고 생각하나요?
7. 동성학교 교육을 시도하는 미국 학교의 학생들이 남녀공학 학교의 학생들 보다 더 공부를 잘 한다고 한다. 이 것은 동성학급 교육이 더 좋다는 것을 뜻하지 않나요? 여러분의 의견은?
8. 학교에서 이성친구와 키스하거나 껴안는 것이 허락되어야 한다고 생각하나요? 그 이유는? 그렇게 하는 것을 막을 수 있을까요? 그렇다면, 어떻게?

3. LEARNING ENGLISH

영어를 배우는 이유

몇년 전 까지만 해도 한국의 학생들은 중고등학교 교과과정으로 영어를 배웠다. 대부분 영어를 읽고 쓰는 교육이 중점이었고 말하기 교육은 받지 않았다.

대학 입학 시험. 그 이유는 학생들이 어려운 대학 시험을 준비해야 했기 때문이다. 영어 말하기 능력보다는 독해력과 문법위주의 시험이었다.

시대의 변화. 그러나 시대는 변해서 요즘엔 유치원생들도 영어를 배우고 있다. 알파벳과 기본 표현부터 배운다. 그 아이들이 고등학교를 졸업할 때엔 원어민과 대화를 할 수 있을 것이다.

오늘날에 영어를 배우는 것은 그 어느 때보다 중요하다. 한국의 많은 기업들은 외국에 수출을 한다. 그래서 한국의 사업가들은 영어를 잘 해야 한다. 현재 영어회화를 초등학교 3학년 때부터 가르치는 이유가 그 때문이다.

영어교육 자료/도구. 요즘에 언어를 배우는 것은 15년 또는 20년 전과는 다르다. 요즘엔 컴퓨터 응용프로그램이나 다른 전자 교육기기를 사용해 쉽고 재미있게 배울 수 있다. 인터넷 사이트에서 영어를 배울 수도 있다. 많은 영어교육 컴퓨터 프로그램은 마치 컴퓨터 게임 같다. 그래서 학생들이 더 재미있게 배운다. 대부분의 학생들은 책보다는 컴퓨터를 가지고 영어를 배우고 싶어 한다.

그 누구도 영어를 말하고 듣는 연습 없이 영어에 유창해질 수 없다. 그렇기 때문에 대부분의 고등학교엔 학생들이 다른 친구들과 연습을 할 수 있는 영어 동아리가 있다.

QUESTIONS FOR DISCUSSION

1. 어린 아이들이 영어를 배우는 것에 대해 어떻게 생각하나요? 왜 그렇게 생각하나요.
   a. 좋은 생각이다. 어린 나이에 시작하는 것이 좋다.
   b. 어린 나이에 영어를 배울 필요는 없다. 한국어를 배우는 것으로 충분하다.
2. 영어를 배우는 것에 대해 어떻게 느끼나요?
   a. 아주 좋아한다. b. 영어가 어려워서 싫다. c. 싫어하지만 영어로 말하는 것은 좋아한다.
3. 영어를 배우는 주된 목적은 무엇인가요?
   a. 배우는 것을 즐긴다. b. 대학 입학 시험을 통과하기 위해서
   c. 미래에 좋은 직장을 구하기 위해서 d. 외국여행을 할 때 사용하기 위해서
4. 컴퓨터 프로그램을 사용해서 영어를 공부한 적이 있나요? 있다면, 어땠나요? 컴퓨터로 영어를 배우는 것을 좋

아하나요? 이유는?

5. 다음의 방법들이 각각 왜 영어를 배우는데 좋다고 생각하나요?
   a. 영어로 TV프로그램이나 영화를 본다.
   b. 원어민과 말하기 연습을 한다.
   c. 회화 연습을 할 수 있는 컴퓨터 프로그램을 사용한다.
6. 학교에서 영어 동아리에 가입하는 것은 중요하나요? 여러분의 학교엔 영어 동아리가 있나요, 그렇다면 회원인가요? 그 이유는?
7. 영어를 쓰는 나라에서 학교를 다니지 않고도 영어를 유창하게 할 수 있다고 생각하나요? 그 이유는?

4. STUDYING FOR TESTS

너무 많은 시험

시험을 보는 것은 한국인들 삶의 일부분이다. 통과해야 할 시험은 끝이 없는 것처럼 보인다.

고등학교 입학. 1997년 이전까지 한국 학생들이 치뤄야 할 첫번째 가장 중요한 시험은 고교 입학 시험이였다. 모든 중3생들은 이 시험을 봐야만 했다. 이 시험을 통해 각각의 학생들이 다닐 고등학교가 결정됐다. 이 시험은 1998년에 중단되었다.

대학 입학. 학생들이 여전히 걱정하는 큰 시험은 "수능" 이다. 대학에 가고자하는 모든 고3들은 이 시험을 봐야한다. 성적은 학생들이 입학할 대학을 결정하는데 사용된다. 서울에 있는 명문 대학에 입학하기 위해서는 이 시험에서 아주 높은 점수를 받아야 한다.

자격증 시험. 시험보기는 대학에 입학한 후에도 멈추지 않는다. 대학 4학년들 중 일부는 직장을 구하기 전에 자격증을 꼭 따야 한다.

회사에 취직한 후에도 정기적인 승진시험이 있다. 그 시험에서의 성적은 한 단계 높은 직급으로의 승진여부를 결정한다.

영어 시험. 그런 시험들 이외에도 대부분의 한국 대학생들과 직장인들이 쳐야만 하는 중요한 두 영어시험, 토플과 토익 시험이 있다. 이 두 시험의 성적은 한 사람이 얼마나 영어를 잘 읽거나 구사하거나, 또는 이해하는지를 말해준다.

공무원 시험 – 한국인이 정부나 정부기관에서 일하기 위해서는 공무원 시험을 쳐야만 한다. 외교관이 되기 위해서나 한국 정부를 외국에서 대표하기 위해서는 외무고시를 통과해야만 한다.

한국인이 무슨 직업을 갖든지 시험을 쳐야 하는 것 처럼 여겨진다.

QUESTIONS FOR DISCUSSION

1. 한국인이 쳐야하는 많은 시험에 대한 여러분의 의견은? 너무 많다고 생각하나요? 왜 그렇게 생각하나요.
   a. 많다고 생각하지 않는다. 시험을 치는 것은 필수적이다.
   b. 너무 많다고 생각한다. 바뀌어야 한다고 생각한다.
2. 여러분은 세계의 모든 사람들이 많은 시험을 본다고 생각하나요? 아니면 한국인들이 더 많은 시험을 본다고 생각하나요? 왜 그렇게 생각하나요.
3. 시험에서 최고의 성적을 거두는 방법은 무엇이라고 생각하나요?
   a. 각 과목을 시험 전까지 조금씩 공부한다.

b. 시험 보기 전 며칠 동안만 아주 열심히 공부한다. 그것으로 충분하다.

4. 시험보기 전날 밤새워 공부하는 것에 대해 어떻게 생각하나요? 그렇게 해 본 적이 있나요? 다시 그렇게 하고 싶나요?
5. 한국의 고교생들은 대체로 대학시험을 앞두고 적은 수면을 취한다. 그것이 좋은 일이라고 생각하나요?
6. 영어회화 능력이 대입시험에 얼마나 중요하나요? 회화 능력이 중요하나요 아니면 읽기와 문법능력이면 충분하나요?
7. 컨닝이 한국의 중.고등학교에서 문제인가요? 몇 퍼센트의 학생들이 컨닝하나요?
8. 대학 시험에 컨닝해서 대학에 들어갈 수 있나요?
9. 의과 대학 시험에 컨닝해서 들어간 의사나 치과 의사가 있다면 그 병원에 가겠습니까? 그 이유는?

5. VIOLENCE NEAR SCHOOLS

십대 불량 학생들

요즘 한국의 학교들은 불과 몇년 전처럼 그렇게 안전한 장소가 아닌 것이 슬픈 현실이다. 일부의 고교생들은 불량 써클에 가입한다. 그런 불량 학생들은 학우들을 구타하거나 돈을 빼앗거나 , 또는 다른 범죄를 저지른다.

때로 그들에게 당한 희생자들은 그 불량 학생들이 무서워 다니던 학교를 그만두고 다른 학교로 전학가거나 심지어 자살하기까지 한다.

살인. 1997년에 충남에서 발생한 잘 알려진 사건이다. 세명의 15세 불량 학생들이 한 급우를 시키는 대로 하지 않는다는 이유로 죽였다. 수영을 못한다는 것을 알면서도 호수에 던져서 그 급우는 익사했다. 그 불량 학생들은 살인죄로 체포되었다.

홈페이지. 오늘날 조직폭력은 한국사회의 큰 문제이다. 인터넷에 학생이나 학부모들이 이메일로 조직폭력을 신고하길 요청하는 홈페이지까지 있다. 한국 경찰은 이런 십대범죄를 뿌리뽑기로 작정했다. 학교주변에 경찰관을 배치하는 일 이외에도 십대 불량배들을 출입시킨 술집, 전화방, 성인전용 오락시설의 주인들을 체포했다.

많은 한국인들은 일본 만화책 때문에 한국의 십대 폭력조직이 증가했다고 생각한다. 그런 만화책들은 십대들이 어떻게 폭력조직을 조직하고 약한 학생들을 괴롭히는지 가르친다. 그런 만화책으로 "파워 클럽" "스피드 건" 같은 것들이 있다. 그런 만화책들은 한국의 십대들에게 아주 인기가 높다.

최근에는 교통법을 어기고 싸움을 일삼고 핸드백을 날취하고 커다란 소음을 일으키는 "오토바이 폭력배들"이 늘고있다.

이유? 왜 불량 청소년들은 다른 급우들의 물건을 빼앗고 급우들을 괴롭힐까? 그건 다른 사람들을 복종하게 만드는 데에서 느끼는 우월감 때문이다. 그렇게해서 자신이 중요하다고 느끼고 싶어한다. 그런 십대들은 부모의 사랑과 지도 감독이 부족하다.

QUESTIONS FOR DISCUSSION

1. 여러분의 학교 주변에 십대 불량배들이 있나요? 만약 그렇다면, 그들은 무엇을 요구하나요? 그들은 큰 문제인가요?
2. 여러분은 다른 학생들을 괴롭히는 십대 불량배들 때문에 학교가기가 두려운 적이 있었나요? 그렇지 않다면, 그런 불량학생들을 두려워하는 친구가 있나요?
3. 여러분은 십대 불량배들에게 피해를 입은 적이 있나요? 만약 그렇다면, 무슨 일을 당했고 언제 그 일이 있었나요?

4. 왜 일부 청소년들은 다른 학생들의 물건을 빼앗고 그들을 괴롭히나요? 왜 그렇게 생각하나요.
   a. 단지 자신이 중요하다고 느끼고 싶어한다.
   b. 쉽게 돈을 마련하는 일이라고 생각한다.
   c. 학교 다니는 것을 싫어하는 나쁜 학생들이다.
5. 누가 그런 불량 청소년 문제의 책임자라고 생각하나요? 부모님들, 선생님들, 또는 그들이 속한 사회. 왜 그렇게 생각하나요.
6. 왜 일본 만화책 출판사들은 청소년들이 그런 나쁜 일들을 저지르게 만드는 책들을 판매하나요? 그들의 판매를 금지시켜야 되나요? 그 이유는?
7. 경찰은 서울과 다른 대도시에서 늘어나고 있는 십대 오토바이 폭력배들에 대해서 어떻게 대처해야 하나요? 경찰이 할 수 있는 일은?
8. 경찰은 다른 학생들에게 폭력을 가하는 불량 십대들을 막을 수 있을까요? 그렇다면, 어떻게?
9. 만약, 각 학교에 경찰을 배치하면 다른 학생들에게 폭력을 가하는 불량 십대들을 막을 수 있을까요? 왜 그렇게 생각하나요.
10. 다른 학생들에게 폭력을 가하는 불량 십대들은 어떤 처벌을 받아야 하나요?

6. SEX EDUCATION

십대 임신

십대 임신이 한국에서 계속해서 커지는 사회문제인 점은 슬픈 사실이다. 십대 부모가 되는 십대의 수가 증가하고 있다.

"십대 엄마" 에 대한TV 다큐멘터리들이 만들어지고 중학생이 임신하여 출산을 하는 내용의 영화가 만들어졌다. 최근엔 한국에서 십대엄마가 되는 것이 흔한 현상처럼 여겨진다. 계속해서 더 많은 수의 십대들이 성경험을 하고 있다.

한국의 중, 고등학교는 성교육을 하고 있다. 그러나 대부분의 교사들이나 전문가들은 성교육 수업 (내용) 이 충분하지 않다고 말한다. 매년 줄어드는 수의 십대가 임신을 하는 반면 늘어나는 수의 십대가 출산을 한다.

안타깝게도, 한국의 교육부에서는 성교육을 필수과목으로 지정하지 않고 있다. 2008년의 통계에 따르면 서울, 인천 그리고 경기도 고교 남학생들 중 단지 60퍼센트만이 일년 평균 약 2시간 반정도의 표준화되지 않은 성교육을 받았다.

십대는 모든 소년 소녀들에게 힘든 시기이다. 이 시기에 처음으로 낭만적인 사랑을 느낀다. 십대들은 또한 성에 대한 아주 강한 호기심을 가지고 있다. 이 시기는 사춘기라 불린다.

그러나 청소년들과 성에 대해서 대화를 나누지 않는 한국의 전통적인 사고방식이 문제이다. 현대 사회에서는 그 사고방식이 통하지 않는다.

인터넷에 포르노가 널려있고 채팅 방은 섹스 파트너를 만나는 장소로 사용되고 있다. 증가하는 숫자의 십대가 섹스를 한고 많은 십대 소녀들이 임신을 하게 된다. 많은 십대 폭력배들이 성범죄를 저지른다.

학교에서 성교육을 받으면 많은 도움이 된다. 그렇지만 대부분의 학교에서는 성교육을 소홀히 하고 있다. 왜 그럴까? 어쩌면 성교육을 받은 학생들이 더 성경험을 하고 싶어한다고 생각하기 때문인지 모른다.

그렇지만, 그런 생각은 근거가 없다고 판명됐다. 미국과 다른 나라에서 실시된 연구 결과 성교육을 받은 학생들이 전혀 받지 않은 학생들 보다 더 적게 섹스를 했다고 밝혀졌다.

문제는, 언제쯤에나 한국의 교육제도는 현실을 따라 잡을까? 이 문제는 한국의 사회 문제로서 계속해서 커지고 있다. 이 문제를 무시한다고 그것이 사라지는 것은 아니다.

QUESTIONS FOR DISCUSSION

1. 여러분의 학교에서는 성교육을 실시하고 있나요? 만약 그렇다면 어떤 학생들이 성교육을 받나요 – 학교의 모든 학생들, 아니면 단지 일부의 학생들? 학생들에게 성교육 수업이 인기가 있나요? 이유는?
2. 다음 중 한국에서 가장 심각한 성문제는? 그 이유는?
   a. 십대들의 섹스　　b. 십대 소녀들의 출산
   c. 십대 소녀들의 매춘　　d. 십대 소년들이 저지르는 강간
3. 다음 중에서 어느 것에 동의하나요? 이유는?
   a. 성교육을 받은 학생들이 더 성경험을 하고 싶어 할 것이다.
   b. 성교육을 받은 학생들은 성경험을 하는 것에 대해서 더 신중하게 생각할 것이다.
4. 만약, 성교육을 실시하는 것이 좋다고 생각한다면, 언제 (몇 살 때부터) 시작해야 가장 좋다고 생각하나요 – 초등, 중등, 또는 고등 학교? 왜 그렇게 생각하나요.
5. 여러분은 부모님들로부터 성교육을 받은 적이 있나요? 여러분은 부모님께 성에 대해 질문한 적이 있습니까? 만약 그렇지 않다면, 왜 부모님과 성에 대해 의논하지 않았나요?
6. 여러분은 성교육이 학생들에게 더 또는 덜 성경험을 하고 싶게 만들 것이라고 생각하나요? 왜 그렇게 생각하나요.
7. 여러분은 년간 2시간 반의 성교육이 충분하다고 생각하나요? 그 시간 동안에 충분히 배울 수 있나요? 년간 얼마의 시간이 성교육에 할애되어야 한다고 생각하나요?
8. 왜 대부분의 학교에서 성교육이 실시되지 않고 있나요?
   a. 중요하지 않다고 생각되므로.
   b. 선생님들이 성교육 하기를 꺼려하므로.
   c. 성교육을 받은 학생들이 더 성경험을 하고 싶어 할 것이라고 생각하므로.

7. PRIVATE INSTITUTES

한국의 학원들

한국정부는 밤 10시 이후의 학원 수업을 금지해야 한다고 믿고 있다. 그 이유는 입시 전문 학원의 학원비가 중산층 가족들에게 아주 큰 부담이 되기 때문이다.

학교와 학원간의 경쟁 – 공립 학교에서도 밤 10시까지 방과후 수업을 가르치는 것이 허락되었다. 그래서 공립학교가, 10시 이후 수강을 더 이상 못하게 될 사설 학원과 경쟁할 수 있게 되었다. 2008년에는 54퍼센트의 고교생들이, 80퍼센트의 중고생들이 학원교육을 받았다.

물론 학원 주인들과 학원 선생님들은 학원 수업시간 수를 줄이는 것에 동의하지 않는다. 그들은 공립학교와 경쟁하고 싶어하지 않는다. 그리고 더 확실한 것은 매달 벌어들이는 수입이 주는 것을 원하지 않는다.

그러나 대부분의 부모님들과 학생들은 학원이 밤 10시 이전에 닫게 되는 것은 좋다고 생각한다. 부모님들은 재정 부담이 줄어서 좋고, 학생들은 집에 일찍 돌아가고 싶어한다.

1980년대 이후 한국의 사설 학원은 논쟁의 대상이 되어왔다. 그 당시엔 정부가 사설 학원을 전적으로 금지하려 했었다. 그 이유는 부유층의 자녀들만이 사설 학원에 다닐 형편이 되었기 때문이다. 그 것은 부유한 가정의 학생들만이 좋은 대학에 입학 할 수 있고 가난한 가정의 학생들에겐 그 기회가 없음을 의미했다. 오늘날엔 그 상황이 다르다.

한국인들은 자녀의 교육을 아주 중요시하여 좋은 학교에 보내기 위해서는 돈을 아끼지 않는다. 한국 교육 제도와 과정에 있어서 학원은 아주 중요한 역할을 한다. 학원을 다니는 것도 중요하지만 수강생들이 "적절한" 학원에 다니는 것 또한 중요하다. 어떤 학원에 다니느냐에 따라서 최고의 대학에 입학할 수 있느냐 없느냐가 결정된다고 믿어지고 있다.

서울 내의 학원들 중 단지 1퍼센트만이 최고의 대학에 수강생을 입학 시킬 수 있는 자격을 갖추고 있다. 일부 학생들은 매일 매일 많은 시간을 투자하여 먼 거리에 있는 그 1퍼센트의 학원에 다니고 있다. 한국 정부는 그런 실태에 제동을 걸고자 한다.

QUESTIONS FOR DISCUSSION

1. 여러분은 사설학원에 다닙니까? 그렇다면, 얼마나 오랫 동안 나녔으며 다니는 이유는? 그 학원에서 배우는 것에 만족하나요? 그 이유는?
2. 여러분은 사설학원에 대해서 어떻게 생각하나요? 왜 그렇게 생각하나요?
   a. 좋은 시험 성적을 받기 위해서 사설학원에 다니는 것은 필요하다.
   b. 사설학원에 다닐 필요는 없다. 학교의 정규수업으로 충분하다.
   c. 단지 영어회화 학원만이 필요하다.
3. 모든 사설학원이 똑 같나요, 아니면 일부 학원이 다른 학원들 보다 더 나은가요? 왜 그렇게 생각하나요.
4. 사설학원이 좋고 나쁜 기준은? 다음의 사항들의 중요성은?
   a. 강사 b. 학생수 c. 학원료.
5. 학원 강사의 좋고 나쁜 기준은 무엇인가요? 훌륭한 강사와 그렇지 않은 강사의 차이점은?
6. 밤 10시 이후에도 진행되는 학원 수업을 중단하는데에 동의하나요? 그 이유는?
7. 학원이 학생들에게서 받는 수강료에 제한선이 있어야 한다고 생각하나요? 그 이유는?
8. 영어권의 나라에 사는 학생들은 사설학원에 다니지 않는다. 한국도 그렇게 되길 바라나요? 그 이유는?

8. CHOOSING A CAREER

전공선택

고교시절이 학생들 자신의 미래를 결정하는 때이다. 대학에 진학하고자 하는 학생들의 가장 중요한 결정은 대학 전공이다. 어떤 학생들에게는 전공선택이 쉽지만 대부분에게는 쉽지 않은 일이다. 어떤 학생들, 가령 수학, 과학, 또는 컴퓨터에 흥미있는 학생들은 자신이 미래에 공학자나 의사가 되고 싶을 것이라는 사실을 이미 알고 있다.

그러나 거의 모든 학생들에게는 대학 전공선택이 그렇게 간단하진 않다. 그 이유는 그들이 많은 것들에 관심이 있기 때문이다. 십대들이 미래의 인생을 위해 자신이 원하는 직업을 선택하는 것은 힘든 일이다.

가까운 과거에는 부모님들이 대체로 자녀의 대학전공을 대신 선택해 주었다. 그 선택의 가장 중요한 요인은 졸업후 벌 수 있는 돈이었다. 자녀의 관심이나 재능은 거의 고려하지 않았다. 의사나 변호사의 수입이 가장 좋았기 때문에 대학의 법학과나 의과는 지원자로 넘쳤다.

대학전공을 선택하는데 또 다른 중요한 요인은 대학 입학시험 성적이다. 만약 점수가 높으면 법학이나 의학을 전공할 수 있었다. 그러나 점수가 낮으면 적은 월급을 받는 직업 관련 학과를 선택해야만 했다.

오늘날엔 상황이 변했다. 미래의 직업이 얼마나 많은 부를 가져다 줄 것인가를 따지는 대신에 대부분의 학생들은 그들의 관심과 적성에 맞는 직업을 선택한다. 자신이 좋아하는 전공을 선택하지 부모님이 좋아하는 전공을 선택하지 않는다.

인생에서 가장 성공한 사람들은 자신의 직업을 즐기는 사람들이다.

QUESTIONS FOR DISCUSSION

1. 여러분은 미래에 어떤 직책 또는직업을 가질 것인지 결정했나요? 그렇다면, 언제 결정했고 이유는?
2. 대학의 전공을 이미 선택했나요? 만약 아직 안했다면, 오떤 분야를 생각하고 있나요? 그 이유는?
3. 대학전공을 선택하는데 있어서 아래의 요인들이 얼마나 중요했나요? 가장 중요했고 가장 중요하지 않았던 것은?
   a. 보수 – 여러분이 그 직업을 가짐으로써 받을 수 있는 돈.
   b. 부모님 – 부모님들께서 여러분의 결정에 미친 영향.
   c. 선생님 – 선생님들의 권유.
   d. 전공의 난이도 – 어려운 전공 vs. 쉬운 전공.
   e. 적성 – 가장 관심이 있는 전공.
4. 여러분이 선택한 직업이 부모님 중 한분의 직업과 비슷하나요 아니면 완전히 다른가요? 부모님의 직업과 같은 직업을 선택하면 유리한 점은 어떤 것이 있을까요?
5. 21세기 한국에서 어떤 분야의 직업이 가장 중요할 것이라고 생각하나요? 어떤 분야의 직업이 가장 보수가 많을까요? 왜 그렇게 생각하나요?
   a. 영어교육 b. 농업 c. 컴퓨터 공학 d. 국제 무역 e. 여행 사업 f. 호텔 사업 g. 할인 매장 상업
   h. 우주항공 i. 공무원 j. 의료업 (의사, 간호사)
6. 여러분이 선택한 직업에 영어능력은 얼마나 중요할까요 – 아주 많이, 약간, 또는 전혀?

9. GOING TO COLLEGE

대학 생활

한국에서 대학에 다니는 것은 미국에서 대학에 다니는 것과는 다르다. 무엇보다, 미국에서는 대학에 들어가는 것이 쉬운 반면 한국에선 매우 어렵다.

미국에는 전국적으로 실시하는 대학 입시가 없다. 미국의 각 대학은 자치적으로 학생들을 선발한다. 한국에선 대학교가 수용할 수 있는 학생수 보다 더 많은 학생들이 대학 입학을 원하기 때문에 경쟁이 아주 치열하다. 입시는 아주 어렵고 일부 학생들은 시험에 통과하지 못한다.

한국의 대학은 입학하기는 어렵지만 졸업하기는 쉽다. 미국의 학교는 입학하기는 쉽지만 졸업하기엔 어렵다. 미국의 많은 대학생들은 성적이 나빠서 중도에 포기한다.

한국과 미국의 대학생들에게 한가지 같은 점은 대학시절이 한 사람의 인생에 있어서 가장 흥미있는 시간이라는 것이다. 많은 것을 배우고 미래를 위해 자신을 준비하는 것 이외에 평생 지속될 소중한 우정을 키울 수 있다.

동아리 활동. 대학교에는 많은 교과과정 이외의 동아리 활동이 (음악 동아리부터 하이킹, 영어, 과학동아리에 이르기까지) 있다. 여러분의 관심사에 따라서 동아리를 찾아 가입할 수 있다.

그러나 대학생활이 동아리 활동과 친구사귀기가 전부는 아니다. 요즘의 어려운 취업시장에서 경쟁을 뚫고 취

업을 하려면 학생들은 더욱 더 열심히 공부해야 한다. 고용주들은 학교 성적이 좋지 않은 학생을 고용하려 하지 않기 때문이다.

대학생들은 고교생들 보다 스스로의 결정을 내리는데 더 많은 자유가 있다. 대학생들은 공부하는 시간과 노는 시간을 스스로 선택한다. 많은 대학생들이 그 선택을 잘못하여 노는데에 시간을 더 많이 보내고 결국엔 학업을 중도에 포기하거나 퇴학 당하기도 한다.

QUESTIONS FOR DISCUSSION

1. 여러분은 대학에 갈 예정인가요? 그렇다면, 어떤 대학에 다니고 싶나요? 이유는?
2. 어떤 대학에 다니느냐가 중야한가요? 왜 그렇게 생각하나요.
3. 어떤 대학이 다른 학교들 보다 높은 대학 평가를 받는 이유는 무었인가요? 어떤 것들이 높은 평가에 영향을 미치나요?
4. 여러분은 모든 고교생들이 대학에 진학해야 한다고 생각하나요? 아니면 일부 학생들만? 그 이유는?
5. 만약 여러분이 첫번째 대학시험에 떨어진다면 어떻게 하겠습니까 – 재수, 유학, 또는 포기? 그 이유는?
6. 미국의 많은 대학생들은 학비를 벌기 위해 파트타임으로 일을 한다. 여러분은 한국 학생들도 그렇게 해야 한다고 생각하나요? 이유는?
7. 한국의 대학생들 보다 더 많은 수의 미국 대학생들이 (성적 부진으로) 퇴학을 당한다. 그것은 한국 대학생들이 공부를 더 열심히 하기 때문인가요 아니면 미국의 학교가 더 어렵기 때문인가요? 왜 그렇게 생각하나요.
8. 외국에서 대학에 다니면 좋은 점이 있나요? 그 이유는?
9. 대학생들은 몇퍼센트의 시간을 스포츠와 사교생활에 할애해야 하나요? 왜 그렇게 생각하나요.
   a. 10퍼센트 또는 이하. 대학은 공부하는 곳이지 노는 곳이 아니니다.
   b. 30퍼센트. 공부가 더 중요하지만 열심히 노는 것도 중요하다.
   c. 80 퍼센트. 대학에 다니는 주된 이유는 사교생활과 노는 것이다.

10. STUDYING ABROAD

한국 유학생들

한국에서 대학에 가지 않고 외국에서 대학을 다니는 것이 일반화 된 것은 90년대 중반이다. 한국의 신문기사에 따르면 1996년에는 유학생의 수가 약 2000 명이 넘었으나 2008년의 통계에는 유학생의 수가 216,827명이었다. 그 중의 70퍼센트는 미국 유학생이었다. 2009년에는 원화의 약화로 많은 유학생들이 귀국해야만 했다.

그렇지만, 한국에서 대학에 다니는 것과 유학 중에서 선택을 할 수 있다면 대부분의 대학생들은 유학을 선택할 것이다. 그 이유로는 두가지가 있다.

한국 대학 보다는 외국의 대학 입학이 쉽다. 매년 대학 입시에 응시생의 반이 탈락한다. 그들의 많은 수가 재수를 하기보다는 외국 대학에 입학한다.

영어가 성공의 열쇠이다. 세계화의 시대에 영어를 잘하는 사람들이 좋은 직장을 구한다. 한국어만 해서는 더 이상 좋은 직장을 구하기 힘들다.

하지만, 유학을 아무나 할 수 있는 것은 아니다. 유학은 많은 비용이 든다. 그래서 충분한 유학 비용이 있는 사람들 만이 할 수 있다. 그 뿐 아니라 토플 성적이 좋아야 외국의 학교에 입학 할 수 있다.

외국 여행을 해보지 않은 학생이라면 외국 생활에 적응하는 일이 어려울 수 있다. 다른 풍습과 음식에 적응하는 일이 문제가 될 수 있다. 특히 유학 초기에 친구를 사귀는 일은 어려울 수 있다. 가까운 친구 없이 면 타지에서의 생활은 아주 외로울 수 있다.

새로운 자유. 하지만, 유학 초기에 그곳 생활에 잘 적응만 하면 한국에서 생활하는 것 보다 더 좋을 수 있다. 한국에서 보다 더 자유롭게 자기 생각을 표출할 수 있다. 주변의 시선을 의식하지 않고 입고 싶은 아무 옷이나 입을 수도 있다.

아시아 인들은 다른 사람들을 많이 의식하지만 서양인들은 별로 의식하지 않는다. 외국 문화 속에서 한국에서 보다 더 자유롭게 살다보면 한국으로 돌아가고 싶지 않게 된다.

QUESTIONS FOR DISCUSSION

1. 주변에 유학간 사람이 있나요? 그렇다면, 누구인가요? 떠난 목적은?
2. 한국과 외국 중 어디에서 대학을 다니고 싶나요? 그 이유는?
3. 만약 여러분이 유학을 하고 있다면 다음 중에서 어떤 것이 가장 힘들까요? 왜 그렇게 생각하나요.
   a. 친구 사귀기　　b. 향수병 (가족과 친구가 너무 그립다)
   c. 음식에 적응하기　　d. 항상 영어로 말하기
4. 만약 여러분이 유학을 하고 있다면 가장 흥미로운 일은 무엇일까요? 왜 그렇게 생각하나요.
   a. 한국말을 할 줄 모르는 사람들을 만나는 일　　b. 항상 영어로 말하기
   c. 낯선 곳에 여행하며 견문 넓히기　　d. 새로운 풍습과 사고방식을 배우기
5. 외국에서 사는 것이 한국에서 사는 것 보다 더 쉬울까요? 의논하세요.
   a. 자신의 의견을 솔직하게 표출하기—하고 싶은 말을 자유롭게 하기.
   b. 다른 사람을 의식하지 않고 살기.
6. 한국의 학생들이 유학하는 주된 이유는? 왜 그렇게 생각하나요.
7. 어느 시기가 유학하기에 가장 적당한가요? 초등학교, 중고등학교, 또는 대학교 때. 왜 그렇게 생각하나요.
8. 만약 유학의 기회가 주어진다면, 어디에 가고싶나요? 이유는?

11. THE PAINS OF GROWING UP

십대

십대는 힘든 시기이다. 이 시기는 온갖 종류의 문제들로 가득찬 때이다. 십대는 더 이상 어린이도 아니고, 그렇다고 아직 어른도 아니다. 십대들은 자신의 정체성 (자의식) 을 찾으려 한다. 이 힘든 인생의 시기를 청소년기 (*adolescence*) 라 부른다.

신체적인 변화. 십대 청소년의 신체가 성적으로 발달하는 시기를 사춘기(puberty)라 한다. 성적 성숙은 대체로 소녀의 경우 11세, 소년의 경우 13세에 시작된다. 이 시기에 소년들은 젊은 남성으로 성장하고 소녀들은 젊은 여성으로 성장한다. 청소년들의 신체는 14세 또는 15세 즈음에 성적으로 성숙한다. 그건 자신의 아이를 가질 수도 있다는 것을 의미한다.

청소년기는 모든 십대들이 같은 속도로 성장하지 않으므로 고민되는 시기일 수 있다. 어떤 십대들은 친구들 만큼 빨리 성숙하지 않는 것은 아닌지 걱정한다. 친구들은 키가 큰데 비하여 아직 키가 작은 십대들은 그들이 전

혀 성장하지 않을까봐 걱정을 한다.

또 어떤 십대들은 자기가 너무 크거나, 비만이거나, 마르거나, 또는 못생겼다고 걱정을 한다. 모든 십대들은 어떤 무엇인가에 대해서 걱정을 한다.

십대들은 그들의 외모에 굉장히 신경을 쓴다. 그들에게 옷과 머리모양은 아주 중요하다. 대부분의 십대들은 친구들이 입는 옷과 같은 종류의 옷을 입고 친구들과 같은 머리모양을 해야만 한다고 느낀다.

또래 친구들간의 압력 (peer pressure). 십대들은 그들의 또래 친구들에게 인정받기를 열망한다. 그래서 때때로 그들은 그저 친구들을 즐겁해 하기 위해 또는 친구들에게 강한 인상을 주기 위해 어떤 일이든 한다. 그런 일들을 하도록 만드는 것이 바로 peer pressure이다. 때로는 친구들을 즐겁게 하려고 위험한 일을 하는 경우도 있다.

십대들은 새로운 일들을 시도해 보고 싶어한다. 그들은 또한 흥미로운 일들을 열망한다. 그래서 많은 십대들이 술을 마셔보고 담배를 피워 보거나 또는 자신에게 해로운 다른 일들을 해보는 것이다.

자아의 인식 –키가 크고 성적으로 성숙하는 것 이외에도 십대들은 다르게 생각하고 느끼기 시작한다. 가족을 벗어나 가까운 친구들을 사귀고 자신의 사고방식을 갖기 시작한다. 그들은 친구들과 전화하는데 많은 시간을 보낸다.

때로는 그들의 새로운 행동이 가족들과 말다툼을 불러일으키기도 한다. 그러나 이러한 그들의 변화는 정상적인 것이다. 그건 바로 청소년이 독립적인 개체가 되어가는 과정이다.

QUESTIONS FOR DISCUSSION

1. 여러분은 십대 청소년기가 힘든 시기라 생각하나요? 그렇다면, 왜 그렇게 힘들다고 생각하나요?
2. 아래의 사항들이 여러분에게 얼마나 중요한가요? 그 이유는?
   a. 유행하는 옷을 입고 머리스타일을 하는 것　b. 자기 의사결정을 할 수 있는 능력
   c. 다른 학생들과 친구들의 관심을 끄는 것
3. 여러분은 휴대폰을 가지고 다니나요? 그렇다면, 그 이유는?
   a. 휴대폰을 사용하는 것이 재미있고 필요하기 때문에
   b. 어른처럼 느끼고 싶어서　c. 친구들이 모두 가지고 있어서 (peer pressure)
4. 여러분은 친구들과 어떤 (자신에겐) 좋지 않은 일을 함께 해 본 적이 있나요? 그렇다면, 어떤 일? 그 이유는?
5. 여러분은 가끔 부모님과 말다툼을 하나요? 그렇다면 무엇에 관하여 …
   a. 내 복장　b. 내 친구들　c. 내 행동　d. 내 머리 모양　e. 학교　f. 대학 진학
6. 여러분은 항상 부모님의 말씀에 따라 행동하나요? 그 이유는?
7. 나중에 후회한 결정을 해본 적이 있나요? 그렇다면, 그 경험으로부터 배운 것이 있나요?
8. 인생의 시기 –아동기, 고교생, 대학생– 중 어느 시기가 가장 좋은 때라고 생각하나요? 그 이유는?
9. 여러분은 때로 고민하는 일이 있나요? 그렇다면, 어떤 것들에 대해 가장 많은 고민을 하나요?
   a. 내 외모 / 복장　b. 사교 생활　c. 학교 공부 / 대학 진학　d. 다른 어떤 것?

12. FAMILY RELATIONSHIPS

(가족으로부터) 독립

12살 또는 13살까지 아이들의 생활 중심은 가족이다. 부모가 전적으로 자녀들을 돌보아주고 모든 결정을 대신

해준다. 모든 중요한 활동은 가족과 함께 한다. 가정이 아이들 세계의 중심이다.

가족을 벗어난 세상. 그러나 아이들이 십대가 되면 자신의 삶을 가족 밖에서 형성해야 하고 가족을 벗어난 세상을 배워야 한다. 그리하여 가족이외의 사람들과 가까운 대인관계를 형성해가기 시작한다.

이 시기가 되면 부모들은 종종 아이들로부터 소외감을 느낀다. 부모들은 자녀들이 점점 독립적으로 변하는 것을 보게 된다. 부모들은 자녀들이 가족으로부터 분리되어 나가는 것을 깨닫게 된다.

오늘날 한국인들의 삶은 과거와는 굉장히 다르다. 가정이 더 이상 모든 가족 구성원들이 즐거운 시간을 함께 보내는 중심이 아니다. 오늘날엔 집을 벗어나 할 수 있는 흥미있는 일들과 갈 수 있는 장소가 많다.

독립적인 생활. 대부분의 한국 가정은 자가용을, 어떤 가정은 두대를 가지고 있다. 부모들은 모두 일과가 바쁘고 가야하는 곳도 많다. 그래서 오늘날의 십대들은 과거 어느때보다 독립적으로 자랄 수 있는 기회가 더 많아졌다. 그러나 십대들은 집밖에서 흥미로운 자신의 생활을 갖는다고 하여 가족의 중요함을 잊어서는 안된다.

십대들은 고민거리가 많다. 어떤 대는 많은 삶의 고민거리에 부딪혀 주변의 모든 것으로부터 달아나고 싶은 때도 있다. 그러나 때로는 부모나 언니 오빠에게 조언을 구하는 것이 어려운 상황을 극복하는 가장 좋은 방법이다.

가족과 친밀한 십대들은 운이 좋다. 왜냐면 조언이 필요할 때 멀리가지 않아도 되기 때문이다.

QUESTIONS FOR DISCUSSION

1. 여러분의 가족은 몇명인가요 (부모, 형제자매 포함) ? 여러분은 가족들과 사이가 좋은가요? 설명하세요.
2. 여러분에게 형제자매가 있다면 여러분은 몇번째 자녀인가요? 첫째, 둘째, 막내, 기타? 여러분이 첫째 자녀가 아니라면, 첫째 자녀로 태어났으면 좋았겠다고 생각하나요? 그 이유는?
3. 여러분이 자신의 문제로 고민할 때 누구에게 조언을 부탁하나요? 이유는?
   a. 부모님 b. 형제자매 c. 친한 친구나 급우 d. 선생님
   e. 다른 사람에게 조언을 받지 않고 스스로 문제를 해결한다
4. 다음의 주제 중 어떤 것은 부모님과 의논하고 어떤 것은 의논하고 싶지 싶나요?
   a. 친구 b. 학교와 숙제 c. 돈 d. 남자 친구나 여자 친구 e.성과 사랑 f. 흡연 g. 시험에서 컨닝
5. 여러분이 미래에 부모가 되어 자녀를 갖게 된다면 그 아이들과 대화하고 싶지 않은 문제가 있을까요? 어떤 종류의 문제에 대해서, 그 이유는?
6. 여러분은 가족으로부터 독립했다고 생각하나요? 그렇다면, 언제 (몇살 때) 독립을 시작 했나요?
7. 여러분은 어디에서 더 흥미로운 시간을 보내나요 – 집에서 가족들과 또는 집 밖에서 친구들과? 여러분이 즐겨하는 일들은?
8. 몇살 때 처음으로 핸드폰을 가져야 한다고 생각하나요? 왜 그렇게 생각하나요.

13. CHOOSING FRIENDS

친구 선택

고등학교 때 사귄 친구들은 한 사람의 미래를 크게 변화시킬 수 있다. 십대들은 주변의 사람들에게서 아주 쉽게 영향을 받는다. 그래서 한 십대가 어떤 어른으로 성장하는지는 그가 학교다닐 때 어떤 친구들을 사귀었는가에 달려 있다. 그 때문에 십대들은 친구를 현명하게 선택해야 한다.

만약 정직하고 열심히 공부하여 대학 진학을 계획하고 있는 친구를 사귀면 여러분 또한 대학 진학을 목표로

열심히 공부할 것이다. 그러나 담배 피우고 술을 마시고, 공부를 싫어하는 친구를 선택한다면 여러분도 그와 같은 사람이 될 가능성이 높다. 학교 성적은 나빠지고 영어공부를 하지 않을 가능성이 높다.

가장 친한 친구. 모든 고등학교 학생은 최고로 친하다고 여기는 친구가 필요하다. 그 친구는 고민을 들어주고 필요할 때 충고를 해주고 학교 밖에서 함께 놀 수 있는 사람이다.

성장기에는 그런 친구가 특히 중요하다. 십대들은 많은 문제에 부딪힌다. 그런 문제들이 인내하기에 너무 힘들다고 느껴질 때 마음을 편하게 해주고 격려해 줄 수 있는 친구가 꼭 필요하다.

가장 절친한 친구와는 항상 붙어 다닌다. 그들은 학교에 같이 가고 쇼핑도 같이 하고 오랜 시간 동안 전화 통화를 한다.

가장 친한 친구가 어쩌면 형/오빠나 누나/언니 중 한명일 수도 있지만, 대부분의 십대에겐 같은 반 친구다. 그건 주로 학교 친구가 서로의 생활을 더 잘 이해하기 때문이다.

QUESTIONS FOR DISCUSSION

1. 여러분은 가장 친한 친구가 있나요? 그렇다면, 언제 그리고 어떻게 가장 좋은 친구 사이가 되었나요?
2. 가장 친한 친구가 있는 것이 중요하다고 생각하나요? 그 이유는?
3. 가장 친한 친구 한명이 있는 것 보다 여러명의 가까운 친구가 있는 것이 더 좋다고 생각하나요? 왜 그렇게 생각하나요.
4. 여러분은 몇명의 친구가 있나요? 서로 만나면 어떤 일을 함께 하나요?
5. 여러분은 가장 친한 친구와 서로의 비밀을 얘기하나요? 그렇다면, 어떤 미밀을 서로 나누나요?
6. 한 사람이 사귀는 친구를 보면 그 사람에 대해서 많은 것을 알 수 있다고 한다. 이 말에 동의하나요? 그 이유는?
7. 사람들은 언제 가장 절친한 친구를 사귀게 되나요—초등하교 시절, 중고등 학교 시절, 대학 시절, 또는 일을 하기 시작했을 때? 왜 그렇게 생각하나요.
8. 형제자매가 서로 가장 친한 친구가 될 수 있나요? 아니면 가장 친한 친구는 가족 이외의 어떤 사람이어야 하나요? 왜 그렇게 생각하나요.
9. 만약 여러분이 하고 싶은 어떤 일을 가장 친한 친구가 원하지 않거나 그 반대일 경우 여러분은 어떻게 하나요?
   a. 그 일을 하지 않는다
   b. 다른 일을 함께 한다
   c. 서로 각각 하고 싶은 일을 한다.
10. 여러분은 부모님과 여러분의 친구들에 대해서 얘기를 나누나요? 아니면, 여러분이 어떤 친구들을 사귀는지 부모님은 관심이 없으신가요?
11. 만약 부모님이 여러분이 사귀는 친구 중 한명을 좋아하지 않는다면 여러분은 그 친구와 더 이상 어울리지 않겠습니까? 그 이유는?

14. THE OPPOSITE SEX

십대의 사랑

대부분 사람들은 십대에 로맨틱한 사랑의 느낌을 처음 경험한다. 십대들은 매혹적인 누군가를 발견하고 만나고 바로 사랑에 빠진다. 적어도 자신만은 그 느낌이 사랑이라고 생각한다. 십대들이 느끼는 그 감정은 "teenage crush" 라 불린다. 여고생들은 흔히 젊은 남자 선생님을 열렬히 짝사랑한다. 십대들의 짝사랑 (풋사랑) 은 대체로 오래 가지 않는다–다른 더 매력적은 사람이 나타날 때 까지만 지속 된다.

의견의 차이. 십대는 감성적으로 발달하는 시기이므로 그런 짝사랑(풋사랑) 을 하는 것은 자연스러운 것이다. 두 사람이 서로 좋아할 땐 대부분의 시간을 함께 있고 싶어하고, 데이트를 하고 싶어한다.

한국에서는 고교생들이 데이트 하는 것에 대해서 찬반의 의견이 분분한다. 대부분의 고교생들은 데이트하는 것은 괜찮다고 생각하지만 대부분의 부모님들과 선생님들은 그것에 동의하지 않는다.

한국의 십대들은 남자학교 또는 여자학교에 다니기 때문에 이성에 대한 호기심이 아주 많다. 학교 밖에서나 이성을 만날 수 있다. 이성과 함께 시간을 보낼 수 있는 유일한 방법은 데이트이다.

공부를 할까 데이트를 할까? 일부 부모님들은 십대 자녀가 데이트하는 것을 나쁘게 생각하지 않는다. 하지만 그런 부모님들은 예외이다. 대부분의 한국 부모님들과 선생님들은 고등학생이 좋은 대학에 가길 원한다면 공부에 전념해야 한다고 생각한다. 그분들은 데이트를 많이 하는 학생은 대학입시에서 좋은 점수를 받을 수 없다고 생각한다.

데이트하는 학생들에게 인기 있는 장소는 공원, 극장, 또는 패스트푸드 체인점이다. 그들은 함께 있을 수 있는 한 어디를 가느냐가 별로 중요하지 않다.

QUESTIONS FOR DISCUSSION

1. 여러분은 이성에 대해서 얼마나 많이 생각하나요? 많은 시간, 약간, 또는 전혀.
2. 여러분의 학교가 남녀공학 학교가 된다면 어떨까요? 왜 그렇게 생각하나요.
   a. 공부가 더 재미있을 것이다. b. 공부에 집중하기 힘들 것이다. 동성 학교 (남학교, 여학교 따로) 가 더 좋다.
3. 여러분은 이성친구를 사랑해 본 적이 있나요? 그렇다면, 몇 살 때? 얼마 동안? 그때 기분이 어땠었나요?
4. 여러분은 왜 고교생들이 젊은 선생님을 짝사랑 한다고 생각하나요? 여러분 중에도 그런 짝사랑을 해 보았나요? 그렇다면, 어떤 선생님?
5. 여러분은 사람들이 언제부터 데이트를 시작하는 것이 가장 좋다고 생각하나요? 그 이유는?
   a. 중학교 때 b. 고등학교 때 c. 대학교 때
6. 여러분이 데이트 하는 것에 대해 부모님은 어떻게 생각하나요?
7. 남녀가 데이트할 때 누가 돈을 써야 하나요? 남학생이 모두, 여학생이 모두, 또는 반반씩?
8. 여러분은 여자가 자신보다 더 나이 많은 남자와 데이트를 해도 괜찮다고 생각하나요? 남자가 자신보다 더 나이가 많은 여자와 데이트 하는 것은?
9. 친한 친구들과 어울려 노는 것과 이성의 친구와 데이트 하는 것 중 어느 것이 더 재미있나요?
10. 어떤 학생들은 이성의 친구와 데이트 하는 것 보다 동성의 친구들과 함께 어울리는 것을 선호한다. 그런 친구들에 대해 이상하다고 생각하나요, 아니면 아무렇지 않게 생각하나요?

15. MODERN KOREA

생활방식의 변화

한국은 지난 몇 십년 동안 아주 많이 변했다. 한국은 여러면에서 25년 또는 30년 전과는매우 다르다. 너무 달라져서 다른 나라가 되어버린 것 같다.

오늘날 한국인들은 햄버거와 피자를 좋아한다. 그러나 1988년 올림픽 이전에는 한국에 햄버거나 피자 패스트푸드점이 하나도 없었다.

오늘날 고속도로는 매우 복잡하다. 25년 전에 도로에서 볼 수 있었던 대부분의 차는 택시였다. 오늘날 18세 이상 대부분의 사람들은 면허증을 가지고 있다. 1985년만 해도 단지 소수의 한국사람들만 운전면허증이 있었고 그들은 대부분 남성들이었다.

새로운 쇼핑습관. 한국인들은 이제 과거와는 전혀 다른 쇼핑을 한다. 25년 전에는, 대부분의 한국인들은 식료품에서부터 의류와 전기제품에 이르기까지 거의 모든 물건을 판매하는 시장이라는 개방된 장터에서 쇼핑을 했다. 상품에 가격이 표시되어 있지 않았기 때문에 구매자들은 가게주인들과 더 싼 값을 놓고 흥정을 했다.

오늘날의 한국인들은 필요한 모든 물건을 살 수 있고 가격이 저렴한 이마트 또는 롯데 마트 같은 규모가 큰 할인매장에서 쇼핑을 한다. 한국인들이 노출된 장터를 외면하는데에는 몇 가지 이유가 있다.

첫째 이유는, 거의 모든 사람들이 운전을 하므로 주차장이 필요하다. 시장에는 주차장이 없는 반면에 큰 할인매장에는 있다.

많은 할인매장에는 실내 주차장이 있기 때문에 비오는 날이나 날씨가 추운 날에도 쇼핑하기에 편리하다. 매장안은 겨울에는 따뜻하고 여름에는 시원하다. 그러나 시장은 밖에 있으므로 겨울에 춥고 여름에는 덥다.

할인매장에는 상품선택의 폭이 넓다. 가격은 저렴하고 고객들은 가격 흥정을 할 필요가 없다. 그리고 시장은 밤에 닫는 반면에 대부분의 할인매장은 24시간 영업을 한다.

과거에는 단지 여성들만 식료품을 사러 시장에 갔다. 그러나 요즘엔 남성들 또한 쇼핑카트를 밀고 있는 것을 볼 수 있다. 이젠 남성들이 시장에 가는 것이 보편화 되었다. 80년대에 대부분의 남성들은 슈퍼 (매장) 에서 쇼핑을 하는 것을 챙피하게 생각해서 꺼려했다. 왜냐면 쇼핑은 여성들이 해야하는 일로 여겨졌기 때문이다.

QUESTIONS FOR DISCUSSION

1. 여러분이 어렸을 때 한국은 어땠는지 기억하나요? 그때와 비교해서 변한 것들이 있나요? 만약 그렇다면, 어떤 것들?
2. 여러분은 때때로 패스트푸드점에 가나요? 80년대 처럼 패스트푸드점이 하나도 없다면 좋을까요? 그 이유는?
3. 시장과 할인매장 중에 어디에서 쇼핑하는 것을 선호하나요? 왜 그렇게 생각하나요? 여러분의 어머니는 어디에서 쇼핑을 하시나요?
4. 다음은 25년 전에는 대부분의 사람들이 가질 수 없거나 한국에는 없었던 것들이다. 그러나 현재의 여러분들은 가질 수 있는 것들이다. 만약 우리가 이런 것들을 가지고 있지 않다면 더 행복할까? 그 이유는?
   a. 휴대폰 b. 컴퓨터 c. 인터넷 d. 디지털 카메라 e. DVD players f. 할인 매장 g . 자가용
   h. 케이블 텔레비젼
5. 80년대에 대부분의 남성들은 슈퍼 (매장) 에서 쇼핑을 하는 것을 챙피하게 생각했던 것에 대해서 어떻게 생각하나요? 왜 그렇게 생각하나요.
   a. 내 생각엔 그렇게 생각했던 것이 당연하다. 쇼핑은 여성들의 일이었다.
   b. 그건 말도 안된다. 쇼핑은 모든 사람들이 해야하는 일이다.
6. 여러분은 왜 1980년대에 남자들만 주로 운전을 했다고 생각하나요? 그 이후로는 어떻게 한국인들의 사고방식이 바뀌었나요?
7. 여러분은 한국의 전통시장이 앞으로 어떻게 될 것이라고 생각하나요? 한국에 시장이 존속할까요 아니면 앞으로 언젠가는 완전히 사라질까요? 왜 그렇게 생각하나요.

8. 1980년대엔 거의 아무도 소유하지 않았던 자가용 만큼 한국인의 삶의 바꾸어놓은 것은 없다. 20년 또는 30년전 사람들의 삶과 비교했을 때 자가용의 소유가 현대인의 삶을 어떻게 바꾸어 놓았나요?

16. CITY LIFE, COUNTRY LIFE

시골에서 도시로

한국은 최근에 개발도상국에서 선진국으로 변화하였다. 선진국들은 산업화되었으나 개도국들은 대부분 농업 중심국이다. 30년 전에는 한국인의 대부분이 농업인이었으나 오늘날의 대부분의 사람들은 공장이나 사무실 빌딩에서 일을 한다.

30년 전의 한국 경제는 농산품의 수출이 중심이었으나 오늘날엔 수출품의 대부분이 공산품이다.

빠른 발전. 한국의 빠른 발전은 70년대에 시작되었다. 그리고 그때가 바로 이촌향도 현상이 시작된 시점이다. 농촌생활은 힘들기 때문에 많은 젊은 사람들이 시골을 벗어나 도시로 이동하는 것은 놀라운 일이 아니었다. 도시에서 공장이나 회사에 취직할 수 있었다.

1980년에는 인구의 20%가 시골에서 살았으나 1995년이 되어서는 시골에 사는 사람들의 수는 반으로 줄었다.

젊은 사람들이 시골을 떠나 도시에서 살고자하는 이유는 몇가지가 있었다. 가장 큰 이유는 소득이었다. 농부들은 아주 힘들게 일하지만 돈을 많이 벌지 못한다는 것은 누구나 아는 사실이다. 반면에 공장 근로자들은 적은 시간 일하고 더 많은 돈을 번다.

더 많은 자유 시간. 도시로의 이주의 또 다른 이유는 더 많은 자유시간을 갖기 위해서 였다. 농부들은 쉴 수 있는 자유 시간이 많지 않은 반면에 도시인들은 자유시간을 가질 수 있다. 또한 사교생활을 할 수 있다. 도시에는 즐길 수 있는 일들이 많다. 농부들은 일찍 일어나고 일찍 잠자리에 드는 반면 도시인들은 늦게 잠자리에 들고 늦게 일어난다.

그러나 도시는 소음과 교통혼잡에 시달린다. 또한 자가용과 트럭 그리고 버스때문에 공기가 오염되었다. 시골 마을은 조용하고 공기가 깨끗하다. 그래서 요즘 시골에서 도시로 이주했던 일부 사람들은 아직도 시골에서 계속 살았더라면 좋았겠다는 생각을 한다.

QUESTIONS FOR DISCUSSION

1. 다음중 어디가 가장 살기 좋은 곳이라고 생각하나요? 왜 그렇게 생각하나요.
   a. 대도시　b. 대도시 주변　c. 시골이 가까운 조그만 도시　d. 시골
2. 도시에서는 할 수 있으나 시골에서는 할 수 없는 것은 어떤 것들이 있나요?
3. 도시에서 사는 것보다 시골에서 사는 것의 장점은 무엇이 있나요?
4. 은퇴 후 살기에 더 좋은 곳은 어디인가요? 왜 그렇게 생각하나요.
5. 시골의 큰 집과 대도시 주변에 있는 고층빌딩속의 작은 아파트 중 어디에서 살고 싶나요? 왜 그렇게 생각하나요?
6. 시골과 도시 중 다음의 각각 일들을 하기에 어디가 가장 좋은 곳이라고 생각하나요? 그 이유는?
   a. 쇼핑　b. 죠깅 또는 자전거 타기　c. 고등하교 다니기
   d. 영화보러 가기　e. 친구들과 어울려 놀기　f. 수영 가기
   g. 영어 배우기　h. 운전 배우기
7. 미래에는 도시에 사는 많은 사람들이 거꾸로 시골로 이주할 것이라고 생각하나요? 만약, 그렇게 생각하지 않는다면, 그 이유는? 왜 사람들이 시골보다 도시의 생활을 선호할 것이라고 생각하나요?

17. SAFETY AWARENESS

어린이 안전좌석

어린이용 안전좌석은 어린이를 위한 안전벨트와 같다. 만약 어른들이 차를 타고 갈 때 안전벨트를 꼭 착용해야 하다면 어린이들 또한 그렇게 해야 하지 않나요?

사실은 1990년도 이후 유아와 어린이의 안전좌석 사용이 법으로 만들어졌으나 대부분 한국 부모들은 그 법을 지키지 않는다.

자녀사망의 첫번째 원인. 한국의 차사고로 인한 어린이 사망의 첫번째 원인은 부모님들이다. 그 이유는 자녀들을 안전좌석에 태우지 않기 때문이다.

안전좌석은 차사고의70%의 경우 사망사고를 막아준다. 그리고 67%의 경우 치명적인 부상을 막아준다. 그래서 부모님들이 안전좌석을 사용했다면 매년 차사고로 숨지거나 치명적인 부상을 당하는 어린이들의 대부분은 단지 가벼운 부상을 입는데 그쳤을 것이다.

어떤 사람들은 왜 어린이들이 어른들이 사용하는 안선벨트를 사용할 수 없냐고 질문할 것이나. 또는 왜 아이들을 위해 특별히 만들어진 비싼 안전좌석을 사야하냐고 질문할 것이다.

그 이유는 어린이들이 안전벨트를 차기에는 너무 작기 때문이다. 차 사고가 나면 그 안전벨트가 아이들의 생명을 구하기 보다는 앗아갈 것이다.

부스터 좌석. 4살 이상의 어린이들에겐 안전좌석은 이제 너무 작고 안전벨트는 아직 너무 크다. 그런 어린이들은 이제 부스터 좌석이라는 것이 필요하다. 아이들은 부스터 좌석이 앉는 위치를 높여주므로 일반 안전벨트를 매고 앉을 수 있다.

대부분의 부모님들이 이 법을 지키지 않는 주된 이유는: a) 아이들이 불평해서, b) 안전좌석을 사는데 돈을 쓰기 싫어서, c) 귀찮다고 생각해서, 그리고 d) 경찰이 강력하게 법을 집행하지 않아서이다.

QUESTIONS FOR DISCUSSION

1. 이 장을 (주제를) 공부하기 전엔 어린이 안전좌석에 대해서 어떻게 생각했나요?
   a. 필요하다고 생각했다. b. 불필요하다고 생각했다. c. 들어본 적이 없다.
2. 안전좌석에 대해서 읽고 난 지금은 어떻게 생각하나요? 왜 그렇게 생각하나요.
   a. 모든 아이들은 안전좌석을 사용해야 한다고 생각한다.
   b. 아직도 필요하지 않다고 생각한다.
3. 여러분은 차 안에서 항상 안전벨트를 하나요? 그 이유는?
4. 만약 어른들이 차를 타고 갈 때 안전벨트를 꼭 착용해야 하다면 어린이들 또한 그렇게 해야 하지 않나요? 그 이유는?
5. 대부분 한국 사람들은 안전을 더 많이 생각하나요 아니면 일을 빨리 하는 것에 더 신경을 쓰나요? 여러분은?
6. 한국 경찰들은 왜 안전벨트 착용은 단속하면서 어린이 안전좌석 착용은 단속하지 않나요?
7. 차를 타고 갈때 유아에겐 어디가 가장 안전한 자리인가요? 왜 그렇게 생각하나요.
   a. 유아는 유아용 안전좌석에 앉아야 한다. b. 엄마가 뒷좌석에서 아아를 안고 타야 한다.
8. 여러분의 학교는 안전에 대해서 교육을 하나요? 그렇다면, 학교에 어떤 안전 규칙들이 있나요?
9. 한국은 교통사고가 가장 높은 나라중의 하나이다. 왜 그렇게 많은 교통사고가 발생한다고 생각하나요?
10. 한국은 그런 안전 관련 기록을 개선하기 위해서는 무엇을 해야 하냐요? 왜 그렇게 생각하나요.

18. REUNIFICATION

통일의 큰 걸림돌들

대부분의 남한 사람들의 소원은 북한과의 통일이다. 그러나 통일이 정말 가능한가? 쉽지는 않을 것이다. 두 나라는 각각 매우 다른 정부 (정치구조) 를 가지고 있고, 서로의 정치구조를 비방하기 때문이다.

민주주의 vs 독재주의. 남한은 민주주의 국가이다. 국민에 의해 선출된 대통령이 국정을 담당한다. 북한은 국민이 선출하지 않은 독재자에 의해 법이 만들어지고 통치되는 독재국가이다.

민주주의 국가의 국민들은 자유롭게 이동 (이주) 할 수 있고 외국여행을 할 수 있고 원하는 모든 것을 살 수 있으며, 심지어 그들의 지도자를 비판할 수도 있다.

북한의 국민들은 그러한 자유가 없다. 그들은 심지어 국내여행 조차 허락되지 않고, 모든 뉴스는 검열된다. 그들의 지도자들을 비판한면 죽음을 당하거나 감옥에 보내진다.

남한은 현대화되고 산업화된 국가이다. 남한은 아시아의 부유한 국가들 중 하나이다. 남한 국민들은 컴퓨터를 사용하고, 자동차를 운전하고, 비싼 옷들을 입고, 편안한 아파트나 주택에서 산다.

북한 국민들은 가난하고, 먹을 식량이 부족하고, 전등과 전화기 또는 가전기기가 없는 집에서 산다. 북한을 방문한 적이 있는 외국인들은 북한은 1950년대 이후 전혀 변한 것이 없다고 말한다.

남북한이 분단된지 아주 오래되었다, 그래서 이젠 같은 역사와 언어를 공유한다는 것을 제외하고는 공통점이 거의 없다. 그들의 사고방식과 생활방식은 완전히 다르드.

오늘날 일부 남한 사람들은 북한이 경제적으로 너무 후진국이고 가난해서 통일을 갈망하지 않는다. 통일에 드는 비용은 매우 클 것이고, 남한이 모든 비용을 부담해야 할 것이다.

QUESTIONS FOR DISCUSSION

1. a 와 b 중 어떤 것에 동의하나요? 동의하는 이유는?
   a. 남북한은 서로 같은 역사와 언어를 공유하기 때문에 반드시 통일해야 한다.
   b. 남북한은 서로 사고방식이 너무 달라서 통일을 할 수 없다.
2. 왜 남한이 모든 통일비용을 부담해야 하나요? 왜 북한은 그 어떤 비용도 부담하지 않아도 되나요?
3. 통일 후, 남북한 사람들이 섞여서 살아야 하나요? 아니면 북한 사람들은 따로 분리되어 살아야 하나요? 왜 그렇게 생각하나요.
4. 만약 북한 사람들이 남한 사람들로부터 분리되어 산다면 한국의 사회는 어떻게 변할까요?
5. 통일 후, 일부 남한 사람들은 북한으로 이주할까요? 또는 단지 북한 사람들만이 남한으로 이주할까요? 어떤 남한 사람들이 무엇을 하러 북한으로 이주할까요?
6. 왜 통일의 비용이 클까요? 어떤 것들에 그 비용이 쓰여질까요?
7. 통일 후, 남한에 지금보다 더 많은 인구가 살까요 아니면 남북 전역에 인구가 골고루 퍼질까요? 왜 그렇게 생각하나요.
8. 만약 남북의 벽 (철조망) 이 내일 열린다면, 몇 퍼센트의 북한 사람들이 당장 남한으로 올까요? 왜 그렇게 생각하나요.
9. 일부 남한 사람들은 북한으로 갈까요? 그 이유는?

10. 거리에서 어떤 사람을 만났을 때 그 사람이 남한 사람인지 또는 북한 사람인지 분별할 수 있을까요? 남한과 북한 사람들은 서로 다르게 보이나요 아니면 같은가요?
11. 두 나라의 풍습은 서로 같나요 아니면 다른가요?

19. TEENAGE DEFECTORS

사회 적응

현재 10,000명 이상의 탈북자들이 남한에 살고 있다. 그 사람들 모두 식량과 자유에 굶주려서 남한으로 왔다. 대부분의 북한 사람들에게 삶은 가난과 죽음에 휩싸인 악몽이다. 그들은 자신의 나라에 감금된 죄수들과도 같다.

많은 탈북자들은 남한으로 왔을 때 십대들이다. 그래서 남한의 학교에 다녀야 한다. 물론, 자유를 누리고 굶주리지 않고 좋은 옷을 입지만 남한 사회에 적응하면서 많은 어려움을 겪는다. 가장 가난한 나라중 하나인 북한에서 가장 부유한 나라중 하나인 남한으로의 이동은 쉽지가 않다.

큰 문제점들. 부유하고 현대화된 사회에 적응하는데 어려움을 겪는 것 이외에도 많은 다른 어려움을 겪는다.

1. 건강 문제: 북한에서 굶주림에 시달려서 많은 탈북 십대들은 몸이 아프거나 허약하다.
2. 교육 문제: 많은 수의 탈북 십대들은 북한에서 집이 없이 살며 학교에 전혀 다니지 않았다, 그래서 남한에 와서는 나이가 많이 어린 학생들과 수업을 같이 받아야 한다.
3. 열등감: 대부분의 탈북 십대들은 남한의 급우들 보다 작다 그래서 열등감을 느낀다.
4. 다르다고 느낌: 주변의 사람들이 모두 그들이 탈북 십대라는 것을 안다, 그래서 완전히 동화되기가 힘들다.
5. 너무 현대화된 생활방식: 그들에겐 남한의 부유하고 현대화된 생활방식이 익숙하지 않아 혼란스럽다. 그들은 핸드폰, 현금 자동 지급기, 승차권 자동 발매기, 공중 전화 등등을 본적이 없고 돈을 세는 법도 모른다.
6. 너무 빠른 생활방식: 한국이 아주 현대화된 반면에 한국인의 생활방식은 아주 바쁘고 경쟁이 치열하다. 북한에서의 삶은 조용하고 느리다. 북한엔 거의 차가 없다.
7. 향수병: 자신의 집과 친구들이 있는 곳을 떠나 아는 사람이 아무도 없는 새로운 곳에 서 산다는 것은 쉬운 일이 아니다. 그들은 북한에 있는 가족과 친구들을 아주 많이 그리워 한다.

남한의 학교에 대해서 탈북 십대들이 몹시 싫어하는 한가지가 있다. 남한의 학교에서는 선생님들이 학생들을 체벌하기도 한다. 그러나 북학의 학교에서는 절대로 그런 일이 없다.

만약 북한 사람들이 남한 사회에 동화되지 못한다면 한국 사회는 교육을 잘 받고 부유한 남한인 계층과 그렇지 않은 가난한 탈북인 계층으로 갈라질 것이다. 남한 출신들은 좋은 차를 몰고 좋은 집에서 살지만 북한 출신들은 가난한 지역에서 자전거나 버스를 탈 것이다.

QUESTIONS FOR DISCUSSION

1. 왜 다음의 것들이 각각 탈북 십대들에게 어려운 일인가요? 어떤 것이 그들에게 가장 큰 문제인가요? 왜 그렇게 생각하나요.
   a. 조용하고 가난한 삶에서 바쁘고 부유한 나라에 와서 적응하는 것
   b. 나이가 어린 아이들과 함께 공부하는 것
   c. 핸드폰과 컴퓨터등이 있는 현대화된 사회에서 사는 것
   d. 북한의 가족과 친구들을 그리워 하는 것

2. 만약 여러분이 다른 나라로 이민 갔다면 어떤 것이 가장 큰 문제점 일까요? 왜 그렇게 생각하나요.
3. 여러분은 6살이나 어린 다른 학생들과 한 반에서 공부하고 싶을까요?
4. 여러분의 학교에도 탈북 십대가 있나요? 그렇다면, 그들 중 한명이라도 알고 있나요? 그렇다면, 다음 질문에 대답하세요.
   a. 그들은 많은 친구가 있나요? 다른 친구들이 그들을 다르게 대하나요?
   b. 그들이 외롭다고 생각하나요? 그들과 친구가 되려고 시도해 보았나요? 그 이유는?
   c. 그들은 여러분과 같은 반에서 공부하나요 아니면 다른 반에서?
5. 탈북 학생들이 그들에겐 새나라인 남한에서 행복감을 느끼도록 남한 학생들이 할 수 있는 일은 무엇이 있을까요?
6. 왜 탈북인들을 남한 사회에 적응하도록 하는 것이 아주 중요한 일인가요? 만약 그들이 적응을 못한다면 어떤 사회 문제들이 발생할까요? 왜 그렇게 생가하나요.
7. 얼마나 오랜 시간 (몇 년의 기간) 이 지나야 탈북인들이 자신이 남한 사회의 일부라고 (완전히 적응) 느낄까요?

20. MULTI-CULTURAL KOREA

인종간의 결혼

한국 사회에 큰 변화가 생기고 있다. 한국 사회는 빠른 속도로 다민족/문화 사회가 되어가고 있다. 그 이유는 두가지가 있다: a) 많은 한국 남성들이 외국 여성들과 결혼한다, 그리고 b) 외국인 근로자들이 한국에 살며 한국인들과 결혼을 한다.

그건 한국 사회에도 머지 않아 두 사회 계층이 – 순수 한국인 혈통과 다혈통 계층 – 생긴다는 것을 의미한다. 그런 사회 변화가 일어나면 한국 또한 미국, 캐나다, 그리고 호주와 같이 다민족/문화/혈통의 나라가 될 것이다.

돌이킬 수 없는 변화. 순수 혈통의 인종에서 다혈통으로 변화하는 과정은 꼭 필요하다. 왜냐면 한국인의 남자인구가 여자인구 보다 훨씬 많기 때문이다. 일부 남성들은 외국인과 결혼을 하거나 아니면 결혼을 전혀 할 수 없다.

또한, 한국은 외국인 공장 근로자들을 필요로 한다. 공장에서 일할 수 있는 한국 사람들이 부족해서 다른 아시아 사람들을 채용한다. 만약 외국인 근로자들이 본국으로 돌아가 버리면 일부 공장들은 문을 닫아야 할 것이다.

한국 경제는 외국에 수출하는 자동차와 하이-테크 제품들을 만드는 공장에 의존한다. 만약 외국인 근로자들이 떠난다면 한국 경제는 아주 큰 타격을 입을 것이다.

현재의 추세로는 2025년 이전에 한국은 다혈통 국가가 될 것이다. 초기에 대부분의 다혈통인들은 순수 혈통인들과 많이 다르게 보이지 않을 것이다. 그 이유는 양부모가 모두 아이아 인이기 때문이다.

하지만 그들의 대부분이 이중 또는 더 많은 언어를 유창하게 하기 대문에 쉽게 눈에 띌 것이다. 그들은 한국어를 하고 부모중 한분의 언어도 하고 어쩌면 부모가 서로 영어도 사용하기 때문에 영어까지도 말할 수 있을 것이다.

그렇다면, 한국어와 일부는 영어까지 하는 순수혈통인들 보다 그들이 직장을 구하기가 쉬울 수 있다. 그러나 또 다른 한가지 생각해 봐야 할 것은 순수들이 그들을 어떻게 대할 것인가에 대해서다. 한국인들은 그들의 혈통/배경을 중요하게 생각하기 때문에 다혈통인이 항상 그들과는 좀 다르다고 느껴질 것이다.

그로 인해 한국 사회엔 어떤 문제점들이 생겨날까? 만약 다혈통인들이 삼중언어를 하고 좋은 직장을 차지한다면 다른 사람들은 그들을 질투하고 싫어할 수도 있다.

아니면, 그들이 100퍼센트 한국인이 아니라고 싫어할까? 지금은 알 수 없지만 머지않아 알게 될 것이다.

QUESTIONS FOR DISCUSSION

1. 한국이 다혈통 국가가 되는 것에 대해서 어떻게 생각하나요? 왜 그렇게 생각하나요.
   a. 싫다. 한국 사회가 변하는 것이 싫다.　　b. 좋다. 한국 사회가 더 흥미로워 질 것이다.
2. 순수혈통의 한국인들이 다혈통인들을 어떻게 대할 것이라고 생각하나요? 왜 그렇게 생각하나요.
   a. 다른 한국사람들과 똑같이 대할 것이다.
   b. 외국인처럼 대할 것이다.
3. 한국이 지금처럼 한 언어만을 사용하는 나라에서 여러 언어를 공용어로 사용하는 나라가 될까요?
4. 한국이 다혈통 국가가 되어가고 있다는 것을 많은 한국인들이 인식하고 있나요? 대부분 그것을 좋아할까요 아니면 싫어할까요? 왜 그렇게 생각하나요?
5. 다혈통/민족 국가가 되면 한국인의 음식문화가 변화할까요? 한국인이 먹는 음식이 변화할까요? 식당의 식단이 한국식 뿐만아니라 다민족 음식의 종류를 포함할까요?
6. 다혈통 한국인들은 순수혈통 한국인들 보다 좋은 학교에 들어가는 것이 더 쉬울까요 아니면 어려울까요? 왜 그렇게 생각하나요.
7. 다혈통 한국인들은 순수혈통 한국인들 보다 유명한 회사의 좋은 직장을 구하는 것이 더 쉬울까요 아니면 어려울까요? 왜 그렇게 생각하나요.
8. 다혈통 한국인들은 어디에서 살까요? 왜 그렇게 생각하나요.
   a. 다른 순수혈통 한국인들과 섞여서 함께 살 것이다.
   b. 다른 순수혈통 한국인들과 분리되어 그들만의 공동체에서 살 것이다.
9. 한국이 다혈통/문화 국가가 되면 한국의 풍습과 사고방식이 변화할까요? 그 이유는?
10. 순수혈통 한국인과 3개 언어를 유창하게 하는 다혈통 한국인들 중 어느 그룹이 직장을 쉽게 구할까요? 그 이유는?

21. KOREA'S CAR CRISIS

전기차

전 세계는 석유자원이 줄어들면서 닥칠 에너지 위기를 향해 다가가고 있다. 우리가 사용하는 에너지의 아주 적은 부분만이 태양열이나 풍력으로 생산되고 대부분은 기름을 사용하여 생산된다. 승용차, 버스, 트럭, 그리고 비행기를 움직이는데 그리고 건물의 냉난방에 기름이 쓰인다.

그 에너지 위기는 다른 나라에서 기름을 수입해야하는 한국에게 치명적일 것이다. 기름 생산 국가 (산유국) 들이 더 이상 한국에 수출할 기름이 없다면 어떻게 될까? 한국은 큰 문제에 부딪칠 것이다.

한국 정부는 그 문제에 직면할 때까지 기다리지 않고 한국인들의 운전하는 방식을 바꾸려고 노력한다. 한국 정부는 국민들에게 그들이 현재 주로 구입하고 있는 기름을 많이 먹는 큰 차 대신에 전기차를 구입하도록 권고하고 있다. 현재 전기차가 한국에서 팔리고 있다.

그러나 하나의 문제는, 한국인들은 큰 차를 좋아하는데 전기차들은 아주 작다. 또한, 전기차들은 느리다. 그렇다면, 한국인들은 큰 차 대신에 전기차로 전환할까?

어쩌면 미래에 빨리 달리고 크기가 큰 전기차가 만들어 질 수 있다. 그러나 그것은 먼 미래의 일이다. 한편, 석유값은 계속 오른다. 전 세계의 석유 공급이 감소함에 따라서 계속 오를 것이다.

한국에서 기름값이 계속 오르는 또 다른 이유는 한국인들이 계속 더 큰 차를 사고 계속 더 많은 양의 기름을 사용하기 때문이다. 한국의 운전자들은 에너지 위기에 대해 별로 걱정하지 않는 것 같다.

차 기름값은 얼마? 1997년과 비교했을 때 2010년에는 한국의 차 기름값이 2배 반 이상 증가했다. 그러나 미래에 닥칠수 있는 고유가에 비교하면 그것은 아무것도 아니다.

일부 전문가들에 의하면 앞으로 몇년 사이에 기름값이 250퍼센트 오를 것이라고 한다. 만약 그렇게 되면 한국인 운전자들은 일 리터에 4,000원 이상의 돈을 지불해야 할 것이다.

기름값이 얼마나 비싸야 한국인들은 작은 승용차를 선호하게 될까? 많이 기다리지 않아도 그 답을 알게 될 것 같다.

QUESTIONS FOR DISCUSSION

1. 전기차에 대해서 어떻게 생각하나요? 왜 그렇게 생각하나요.
   a. 좋다고 생각한다. b. 너무 작고 절대로 인기가 없을 것이라고 생각한다.
2. 한국 정부가 국민들에게 작은 차를 사도록 권고하는 것에 대해서 어떻게 생각하나요? 왜 그렇게 생각하나요.
   a. 좋은 생각이다. b. 효과가 없을 것이다. 한국인들은 작은 전기차를 절대 사지 않을 것이다.
3. 다음 중 무엇이 한국인들이 전기차를 사도록 만들까요?
   a. 전 세계의 석유자원이 점점 고갈되어 가고 있다는 사실을 안다면 …
   b. 기름값이 너무 비싸다면 … c. 기름이 완전히 고갈되면 …
4. 얼마나 기름값이 올라야 한국인들은 큰 차를 팔고 작은 차나 전기차를 살까요? 왜 그렇게 생각하나요.
   a. 리터당 3,000원 b. 리터당 5,000원 c. 아무리 기름값이 올라도 작은 차는 절대 사지 않을 것이다.
5. 한국인들은 전 세계의 석유자원이 점점 고갈되어 가고 있다는 것에 대해서 관심이 있나요? 왜 그렇거나 그렇지 않나요?
6. 한국인들이 작은 차 대신에 큰 차를 사는 가장 주된 이유는? 왜 그렇게 생각하나요.
   a. 많은 가족을 위해서 또는 직장의 일 때문에 큰 차가 필요하다.
   b. 친구들이나 이웃들의 부러움을 사고 싶어서이다.
7. 2020년에는 사람들이 크고 작은 차 중에서 어떤 종류의 차를 운전할까요?

22. RECYCLING AND CONSERVATION

재활용을 하는 이유?

모든 선진국 국민들처럼 한국인들 또한 쓰레기를 재활용한다. 재활용은 현세계에 필수적이다. 지구의 천연자원은 고갈되어 가고 있다. 그러므로 모든 사람들은 지구 살리기에 동참해야 한다.

재활용 통. 한국인들은 쓰레기를 버릴때 여러개의 다른 재활용 통에 분리해야만 한다. 대체로 유리병, 캔이나 철제용품, 플라스틱, 종이 등을 담는 통이 하나씩 있고 젖은 쓰레기용의 큰 쓰레기통이 있다.

예전에는 … 재활용이 현재와 같지 않았다. 1990년대에 한국에서 재활용이 시작되기 전엔 모든 쓰레기가 뒤섞여져서 버려졌다. 높은 아파트 빌딩에 사는 사람들은 쓰레기를 낙하시키는 통로로 쓰레기를 버렸다. 그래서 1층에는 쓰레기가 아주 높이 쌓이곤 했다.

그 쓰레기 더미는 악취가 났고 각종 곤충과 쥐들을 끌었다. 오늘날 그런 아파트에 사는 사람들은 모든 쓰레기를 재활용 통에 불리하여 버린다.

재활용을 하면 많은 이득이 생긴다.

재활용은 에너지를 아낀다. 가장 중요한 이득은 재활용을 한 물건들은 다시 사용된다. 재활용을 함으로써 똑같은 물건을 다시 만들지 않아도 되기 때문에 에너지를 80에서 95 퍼센트까지 아낄 수 있다.

재활용은 지구를 살린다. 쓰레기가 분해될 때 메탄 (methane) 이라는 가스가 발생한다. 메탄 가스는 지구 온란화를 일으키는 주 요소이다. 재활용은 메탄가스가 발생하여 지구의 대기속으로 가는 양을 줄인다.

재활용은 천연자원을 보존한다. 종이나 마분지를 만들기 위해서는 나무를 베어야 한다. 나무는 우리가 마시는 산소를 생성하기 때문에 그건 좋은 일이 아니다. 플라스틱을 만들기 위해서는 기름이 필요한데 석유자원은 점점 고갈되어 가고 있다.

우리가 버리는 쓰레기의 조각 조각이 지구 온란화를 일으키는 주 요소가 되거나 소중한 천연자원을 낭비하게 만든다. 이 한가지 만으로도 모든 사람들이 꼭 재활용을 해야하는 충분한 이유이다.

QUESTIONS FOR DISCUSSION

1. 여러분은 재활용이 얼마나 중요하다고 생각하나요?
   a. 아주 중요하다. b. 약간 중요하다. 다른 더 중요한 것들이 있다.
2. 재활용이 어떻게 에너지를 아끼나요?
3. 재활용이 지구의 천연자원을 보존하는데 어떻게 돕나요?
4. 왜 대부분의 한국인들은 재활용을 하나요? 왜 그렇게 생각하나요.
   a. 재활용은 법이라서 꼭 해야하므로.
   b. 재활용은 지구를 살리기 때문에
5. 다음의 것들 중에 어떤 것들은 환경에 해롭고 어떤 것들은 그렇지 않나요?
   a. 종이 가방 (봉지) 이나 박스 b. 플라스틱 가방 (봉지) 이나 병
   c. 상한 음식 d. 오래된 핸드폰 e. 다 쓴 전지 f. 썩은 과일과 야채
6. 왜 일부의 사람들은 재활용을 하지 않나요? 왜 그렇게 생각하나요.
   a. 그들은 재활용의 중요성을 이해하지 못한다. b. 그들은 게으르고 지구 살리기에 관심이 없다.
7. 사람들이 일반도로와 고속도로 주변에 쓰레기를 버리지 못하도록 하는 가장 좋은 방법은 무엇인가요? 왜 그렇게 생각하나요.
8. 도로에 쓰레기를 버리는 사람들은 어떤 처벌을 받아야 할까요? 왜 그렇게 생각하나요.
9. 우리가 버리는 쓰레기의 양을 줄이는 가장 좋은 방법은 무엇인가요? 그런 방법들을 실행에 옮기고 있나요?

23. WORLD POPULATION

식량 생산

세계 인구는 현재 약 70억이고 2025년까지 두배로 증가할 것이라고 전망된다. 매년마다 8천5백만명 정도의 인구가 전년에 비해 늘고 있다. 매년 인구는 1.7 %씩 증가한다. 그러므로 현재의 세계인구 1,000명당 다음해에는 1,017명으로 늘어날 것이다.

지구는 그렇게 많은 사람들을 부양할 수 있을까? 그 모든 사람들을 위한 식량은 충분할까? 지난 세기 이전에는 세계인구의 증가는 걱정거리가 아니었다. 그 이전의 시대에는 사람들이 오래 살지 못했기 때문이다. 100년 전

의 사람들은 약 50년 밖에 살지 못했다.

그러나 현대 과학과 의학의 진보 덕분에 사람들은 80세 또는 90세 이상을 산다. 과학자들은 늘어나는 인구를 먹일 식량을 생산하는 새로운 방법을 발견하기 위해 열심히 연구한다.

그러나 세계인구에 대한 뉴스가 모두 부정적인 것은 아니다. 2000년 이후에는 인구 증가율이 감소하고 있다. 그리고 만약 이것이 지속된다면 2050년에는 세계인구 또한 감소하기 시작할 것이다.

한국은 신생아의 출산이 부족한 나라중의 하나이다. 만약 한국의 가족들이 가까운 미래에 출산을 늘리기 시작하지 않으면 2020년 즈음엔 한국의 인구가 감소하기 시작할 것이다. 그래서 한국 정부는 두자녀 이상을 갖는 가족에 세금감면을 주고 있다.

그러난 인도와 중국을 포함한 몇몇 나라들은 반대의 문제에 – 너무 많은 신생아의 출산 – 직면하고 있다. 중국은 "한 자녀갖기" 운동을 벌이고 있다. 정부는 한 가정이 한자녀만 낳도록 권고하고 있다. 만약 한자녀 이상을 낳으면 그 가족은 더 많은 세금을 내야만 한다.

많은 사람들은 과잉 인구증가가 크게 걱정할 문제가 아니라고 생각한다. 왜냐하면 세계에는 많은 사용되지 않는 땅이 있기 때문이다. 남미와 북미와 같은 곳의 예로, 25퍼센트의 땅만이 농지, 주거지, 그리고 도로로 사용되고 있다. 그 나머지 75퍼센트는 사용되지 않고 있다.

QUESTIONS FOR DISCUSSION

1. 여러분은 세계 인구문제가 우려할 만큼 심각하다고 생각하나요? 왜 그렇거나 그렇지 않나요?
2. 여러분은 자녀가 많은 가족에 세금면제 혜택을 주는 것이 좋은 방침이라고 생각하나요? 왜 그렇거나 그렇지 않나요?
3. 왜 한국은 가까운 미래에 인구가 감소할 수 있는 상황에 있나요? 왜 한국인들이 과거에 비해 적은 수의 자녀를 갖나요?
4. 왜 감소하는 인구 대신에 증가하는 인구가 중요한가요? 만약 한국의 인구가 아주 많이 감소한다면 어떤 문제들이 발생할까요?
5. 중국 정부가 많은 자녀를 두는 가족에 더 많은 세금을 부과하는 것이 정당하다고 생각하나요? 왜 그렇거나 그렇지 않나요?
6. 부유한 나라보다 가난한 나라에서 인구가 더 빨리 증가한다. 왜 가난한 나라 사람들은 더 많은 아이들을 갖는다고 생각하나요?
7. 너무 많은 인구로 도시가 복잡해지면 많은 문제점들이 발생한다. 다음 중에서 가장 심각한 문제점은?
   a. 범죄 b. 공기오염 c.교통문제 d. 식량부족 e. 식수부족 f. 소음문제
8. 세계는 식량문제에 부딪히게 될까요? 왜 그렇거나 그렇지 않나요?
9. 세계에는 사용되지 않고 있는 땅이 많이 있음에도 불구하고 왜 그것이 식량부족 방지를 보장할 수는 없나요?
10. 재활용과 절약 (보존)이 세계 식량고갈 문제를 막는데 어떤 도움을 줄까요? 왜 그렇게 생각하나요.

24. FAST FOOD

버거와 피자

한국에는 햄버거, 피자, 프라이드 치킨, 도넛, 그리고 아이스크림을 살 수 있는 많은 서양식 패스트 푸드점이

있다.

한국에서 가장 인기가 좋은 패스트 푸드점은 외국회사의 체인점들이다. 맥도날드와 버거킹이 88올림픽 바로 전인 1987년에 한국에서 최초로 문을 연 외국 패스트푸드 체인점들이었다.

그 뒤를 곧 피자헛, 던킨 도넛, 웬디스, 윈첼스 도넛, 켄터키 프라이드 치킨, 데어리 퀸 그리고 로테리아가 따랐다. 이 전문점들은 이제 한국 전국에서 찾아볼 수 있다. 심지어 쇼핑몰이나 백화점 안에도 있다.

한국인의 패스트푸드에 대한 입맛이 증가함에 따라 사람들의 체중 또한 증가했다. 패스트푸드가 한국에 소개되기 전에는 사람들이 오늘날 보다 더 날씬했다. 그건 바로 거의 모든 패스트푸드에는 지방, 당분, 또는 둘 다가 너무 많기 때문이다.

오늘날 한국 전역에 아주 많은 패스트푸드 점들이 있어서 1988년 이전에는 하나도 없었다는 사실이 믿겨지지 않는다.

오늘날 패스트푸드 점이 한국의 중고등학생들이 친구들과 만나는 곳이다. 그들에겐 패스트푸드 점이 없는 세상은 상상할 수 없다.

사람들은 패스트푸드 점이 셀프서비스라서 좋아한다. 여러분을 귀찮게 하거나 나가라고 하는 웨이터나 웨이트리스가 없다. 그래서 음료수 하나만 마시며 식탁에 원하는 만큼 오래 앉아 있을 수 있다. 다른 일반 웨이터가 있는 식당에서는 불가능한 일이다. 식사가 끝나면 자리를 떠나야 한다.

불행하게도, 패스트 푸드의 한가지 나쁜 점은 건강에는 좋지 않다는 것이다. 햄버거, 도넛 그리고 프라이드 치킨을 많이 먹는 사람은 살이 많이 찐다.

패스트 푸드에는 영양가가 많지 않다. 그렇지만 우리는 그냥 먹는다. 우리는 많이 먹으면 살이 찐다는 것을 알면서도 왜 멈추질 못하는 것일까? 그건 맛이 너무 좋기 때문이다!

QUESTIONS FOR DISCUSSION

1. 얼마나 자주 패스트푸드를 먹나요? 가장 좋아하는 종류는? 그 이유는?
2. 친구들과 때때로 패스트푸드점에 가나요? 만약 패스트푸드점이 없다면 어디에서 친구들을 만날까요?
3. 여러분은 패스트푸드 점들 중 몇개나 알고 있나요? 그곳에서는 어떤 종류의 음식을 판매하나요? 그 중 어떤 것들을 주로 즐겨 먹나요?
4. 패스트푸드를 먹을 때 그 것이 건강에 좋은지 조금이라도 생각해 보나요? 여러분은 건강에 신경쓰나요? 왜 그렇거나 그렇지 않나요?
5. 왜 한국의 많은 어린이들과 십대들은 그들의 부모님들 보다 패스트 푸드를 더 좋아하나요? 왜 그렇게 생각하나요.
6. 다음 한국의 패스트푸드 중 여러분이 자주 먹는 음식은? 어떤 것이 영양가가 많고 어떤 것은 그렇지 않나요?
7. 왜 패스트푸드가 일반 식당에서 주문하는 음식 보다 영양가가 적나요? 왜 영양가가 높은 패스트푸드를 만들 수 없나요?
8. 방과후 배가 고플때 여러분은 다음중 어떤 것을 먹을까요? 그 이유는?

25. DEADLY CIGARETTES

담배에 중독되기

성인 흡연자들은 줄어드는 반면에 흡연을 시작하는 십대의 수는 늘고 있다. 십대 흡연자들은 똑똑하지 않다.

왜냐면 무언가가 잘못되어 있다는 것을 깨닫지 못하고 있기 때문이다. 어른들이 금연을 하는데에는 어떤 이유, 아주 나쁜 이유가 있어서기 때문이다. 사람들은 아무 이유없이 무언가를 중단하진 않는다.

십대가 흡연을 시작하는 주된 세가지 이유는: a) 호기심, b) 어른처럼 행동하고 싶어서, 그리고 c) 담배가 해롭지만 그들의 몸은 강해서 이겨낼 수 있다는 생각 때문이다.

십대들은 인생은 아주 길다고 느끼고 그들에겐 아무 일도 일어나지 않을 것이라고 생각한다. 또한 병에 걸린다는 생각은 전혀 하지 않는다. 하지만 흡연의 진실에 대해서 알았을 때는 이미 너무 늦었다. 그들은 이미 담배에 중독이 되었다.

십대들은 참을성이 없다. 빨리 자라서 어른이 되고 싶어 한다. 그들은 그 하나의 방법이 담배를 피우는 것이라고 생각한다.

흡연이야말로 사람이 자신의 몸에 할 수 있는 최악의 행위이다. 담배는 이 세상에서 판매되는 상품 중 적절하게 사용되었을 때 죽음을 초래할 수 있는 유일한 것이다.

문제는 어린이들과 십대들은 자신의 몸이 아주 강해서 뭐든지 이겨낼 수 있다고 생각하는 것이다. 또한 언제든지 쉽게 끊을 수 있을 것이라고 생각한다.

그건 참 슬픈 일이다. 왜냐면 담배에는 중독성이 강한 니코틴 성분이 있다. 우리 몸이 그 성분에 충분히 익숙해 지면 그 것을 계속 필요로 하기 시작한다. 그래서 흡연을 하는 사람들이 끊을 수 없는 것이다. 그들의 몸이 계속 필요로 하기 때문이다.

현재의 십대 흡연자들 중 약 절반은 암이나 흡연으로 발생되는 질병으로 죽게 될 것이다. 또한 흡연은 우리 환경과 폐에 더러운 습관이다. 또한 치아를 노란색으로 만들고 나쁜 입냄새를 풍기게 만든다.

QUESTIONS FOR DISCUSSION

1. 흡연에 대해서 어떻게 느끼나요? 왜 그렇게 생각하나요.
   a. 몸에 해롭다. 흡연을 해선 안된다.　　b. 괜찮다. 원하면 해도 된다.
2. 다음 중에서 어떤 것들이 흡연을 해서는 안되는 중요한 이유인가요? 각각을 토론하세요.
   a. 십대들은 흡연해선 안된다.　　b. 흡연이 폐를 검게 만든다.
   c. 흡연이 암을 유발한다.　　d. 흡연이 치아를 노랗게 만든다.
   e. 흡연이 입냄새를 나쁘게 만든다.　　f. 흡연이 환경에 나쁘다.
3. 담배를 피우는 십대들에 대해서 어떻게 생각하나요? 그들은 모두 불량학생들 인가요 아니면 착한 학생들도 있나요? 왜 그렇게 생각하나요.
4. 여러분 학교의 몇 퍼센트의 학생들이 담배를 피우나요? 그것을 어떻게 아나요? 그들은 어디에서 담배를 피우나요?
5. 착한 학생이 담배를 피우기도 하나요? 일부 착한 학생들도 담배를 피우나요 아니면 모두 불량학생들 인가요?
6. 대부분의 흡연을 하는 십대들이 담배를 피우기 시작하는 이유는 무엇이라고 생각하나요?
   a. 어른스럽게 보이고 싶어서.
   b. 위험한 것들을 하는 것을 좋아해서.
   c. 다른 이유 때문에.
7. 불량 써클에 가입한 십대 중에 담배를 피우지 않는 사람이 있나요? 만약 없다면, 그 이유는?
8. 21세가 넘으면 담배를 피워도 되나요? 왜 그렇거나 그렇지 않나요?

26. LIFE IN THE 21ST CENTURY

첨단 미래사회

25년 또는 30년 후의 세상이 과연 어떻게 변해 있을지는 그 누구도 자신있게 말할 수 없지만 첨단기술의 세계가 될 것이라는 것은 확신할 수 있다. 우리가 지금 사용하고 있는 자동차, 컴퓨터 그리고 전화와 같은 것들은 현재의 것과는 매우 다르게 보일 것이다.

아마 일반 가정도 다르게 보일 것이고 우리들은 아직 발명되지 않은 많은 첨단 기기들을 사용하고 있을 것이다.

현재의 기술이 빠르게 발전하고 있으므로 우리는 미래는 최첨단 사회가 될 것이라는 것을 알 수 있다. 지금은 당연히 존재하는 것으로 여겨지는 두가지, 핸드폰과 인터넷은 가까운 과거에만 해도 존재하지 않았다.

초기에는 월드 와이드 웹이라고 불렸던 인터넷은 1992년 이전에는 존재하지 않았고 1995년이 되어서야 세계 사람들이 사용하기 시작했다. 그때가 바로 윈도우스에 웹 브라우저가 포함되어 판매되었던 때이다. 2000년 즈음에는 인터넷은 삶의 필수품이 되었다.

현재 가장 많이 사용되는 첨단기술 기기들은 핸드폰, 컴퓨터, 화상통화, 그리고 평면 텔레비젼이다. 그런 것들이 없다면 살아가기가 힘들 정도로 우리 삶의 필수품이 되었다.

핸드폰. 미래의 핸드폰은 단지 전화를 걸고, 음악을 듣고, 또는 게임을 하는 기능 이상의 다른 기능을 가질 것이다. 여러분의 핸드폰 번호는 변하지 않는 여러분의 주민등록 번호와 같을 것이다. 모든 사람들이 갖게 될 것이고 전화선으로 연결된 집전화는 사라질 것이다.

화상통화. 핸드폰으로 화상통화를 할 수 있는 날이 멀지 않았다. 또한 종이로 된 책이 사라지고 컴퓨터나 전자기기를 통해 책을 읽을 것이다.

컴퓨터와 평면 텔레비젼. 우리들은 현재 커다란 LCD와 LED 텔레비젼을 사서 벽에 걸 수 있다. 그러나 머지않아 스크린이 벽 전체를 가릴 것이다. 한편, 컴퓨터는 더욱 더 잘아질 것이다. 이미 초소형 컴퓨터가 사용되고 있다.

QUESTIONS FOR DISCUSSION

1. 다음의 첨단 전자제품/기기들 없이 살 수 있을까요? 만약 없어도 행복할까요? 왜 그렇거나 그렇지 않나요?
   a. 핸드폰 b. 컴퓨터 c. 평면 화면 텔레비전 d. MP3 플레이어 e. DVD플레이어 f. 인터넷
2. 종이로 된 책 또는 초소형 컴퓨터에서 볼 수 있는 책 중 어떤 책을 읽겠습니까? 그 이유는?
3. 인터넷을 통해 화상통화를 해 본 적이 있나요? 일반 전화와 비교해서 화상통화가 가장 좋은 점은 무엇인가요?
4. 매번 전화할 때마다 상대방이 여러분의 얼굴을 볼 수 있다면 좋을까요? 왜 그렇거나 그렇지 않나요?
5. 인터넷 시대 이전에는 사람들이 어떻게 소식을 주고 받았나요? 인터넷이어떻게 사람들의 통신 수단을 더 편리하게 만들었나요?
6. 학생들이 초소형 컴퓨터를 교실에 가지고 들어오는 것이 허락되어야 하나요? 왜 그렇거나 그렇지 않나요?
7. 지난 15년 동안 다음중 어떤 것들이 가장 많이 변화되었나요?
   a. 텔레비전 b. 전화기 c. 컴퓨터 d. 음악 감상 전자제품
8. 여러분은 호주머니에 들어가는 초소형 컴퓨터를 갖고 싶나요? 왜 그렇거나 그렇지 않나요?
9. 학생들이 핸드폰이나 컴퓨터를 교실에서 사용하는 것이 허락되어야 하나요? 왜 그렇거나 그렇지 않나요?
10. 다음중 어떤 것들이 다음 20년 동안 가장 많이 변화될 것이라고 생각하나요? 왜 그렇거나 그렇지 않나요?
    a. 컴퓨터 b. 핸드폰 c.인터넷 d.CD 와 DVD

27. CELLULAR PHONES

삶의 변화시키는 것들

핸드폰 보다 개인간의 통신수단을 더 많이 바꾸어 놓은 것은 없다. 거의 대부분의 사람들이 핸드폰을 가지고 있다. 우리 일상생활에 꼭 필요해서 없으면 곤란을 겪을 것이다. 놀라운 사실은 단지 2000년도 즈음부터 핸드폰을 사용하기 시작했다는 사실이다. 단지 몇년 만에 우리 삶에 필수품이 되었다.

2000년 이전만 해도 핸드폰을 소유한 사람이 거의 없었다. 일부 사업가들이나 사용했다. 그러나 그때의 핸드폰은 오늘날의 것과는 비교할 수 없다. 그때의 핸드폰은 아주 크고 무거워서 호주머니에 가지고 다닐 수가 없었다. 또한, 성능이 지금처럼 좋지 않았다. 어떤 때는 상대방이 하는 말을 들을 수 없거나 내가 하는 말을 상대방이 들을 수 없었다.

핸드폰이 있기 전에는 호출기가 있었다. 호출기에 전화를 걸 (호출할) 수는 있었으나 상대방과 호출기를 통해 통화는 할 수 없었다. 호출을 받은 사람이 전화번호를 보고 일반 전화로 다시 전화를 해야만 했다.

약속 못지키기. 호출기가 있기 전에는 약속을 못지키는 일이 흔한 일이었다. 교통체증 때문에 주로 늦을 수 있기 때문에 친구들과 만날 시간을 정확하게 세우기가 힘들었다. 차가 막혀 늦는다고 친구들에게 알릴 수 있는 방법이 없었다. 친구는 기다리다 지쳐 집으로 돌아갈 것이고 마침내 도착해 보면 친구는 벌써 떠나고 그 자리에 없다.

오늘날엔 우리 모두가 핸드폰을 가지고 있기 때문에 그런 안타까운 일은 더 이상 일어날 수 없다. 우리는 단순히 전화를 해서 기다리라고 말하면 된다. 기다림에 지쳐 화가 나는 사람은 이제 없다. 핸드폰은 우리 삶을 바꾸어 놓았다.

핸드폰은 아주 짧은 시간에 아주 많이 변했고 앞으로도 더 많이 변할 것이다. 다음 세대 핸드폰은 버튼이 없을 것이다. 모두 터치 스크린이고 아주 가벼울 것이다.

QUESTIONS FOR DISCUSSION

1. 여러분은 핸드폰을 가지고 있나요? 그렇다면, 갖게 된지 얼마나 되었나요? 갖게된 주된 이유는?
2. 우리가 핸드폰을 더 이상 사용할 수 없다면 우리 생활이 어떻게 변화할까요?
3. 여러분의 가족 중 몇명이 핸드폰을 가지고 있나요? 누가 가장 많이 사용하고 어떤 목적으로 사용하나요?
4. 몇살 때부터 핸드폰을 소유해야 하나요? 예를 들어, 8살 어린이가 핸드폰을 사용해야 하나요? 왜 그렇거나 그렇지 않나요?
5. 어떤 경우에 핸드폰이 일반 가정 전화보다 좋은가요?
6. 만약 여러분이 다음 중 하나만 선택하고 나머지는 포기해야 한다면 어떤 것을 선택할까요?
   a. 핸드폰 b. 컴퓨터 c. MP3 플레이어 d. 인터넷
7. 새 핸드폰을 살때 다음 중 어떤 것들이 중요하고 중요하지 않나요? 그 이유는?
   a. 전화 걸고 받기 b. 텍스트 메세지 보내기 c. 음악 듣기 d. 게임 e. 영화 보기 f. 인터넷 사용
8. 핸드폰이 낡아 더 이상 사용할 수 없으면 어떻게 해야 하나요? 그냥 버려야 할까요? 왜 그렇거나 그렇지 않나요?
9. 얼마나 자주 핸드폰을 교체해야 하나요? 왜 그렇게 생각하나요.
10. 학생들이 핸드폰을 교실에서 사용하는 것이 허락되어야 하나요? 왜 그렇거나 그렇지 않나요?

28. THE NEW ANIMATION

컴퓨터로 제작된 영상

컴퓨터 기술의 진보로 애니메이션 분야에 새로운 변화가 일어났다. 오늘날의 애니메이션은 1928년에 제작된 최초의 미키마우스 만화영화에 비하면 100배는 더 뛰어나다. CGI라고 불리고 컴퓨터로 제작된 영상의 단축어다.

더 이상 만화가들이 만화영상의 한장면 (frame) 한장면을 손으로 그릴 필요가 없다. 이젠 그 모든 것이 컴퓨터상에서 이루어지고 영상물은 손으로 그려진 것처럼 보이지 않고 실물처럼 보인다.

CGI 애니메이션이 이전의 애니메이션 만화영화 보다 더 인기가 많다. 단지 어린이들이나 신데렐라 같은 영화를 보고 싶어 하는 반면 어른들도 아이들 만큼 CGI 영화는 보고 싶어한다. 요즈음의CGI 영화는 단지 아이들만을 대상으로 만들어지지 않고 모든 사람들을 대상으로 만들어 진다.

왜CGI 영화가 주류 (mainstream) 가 되었는지 그 이유를 쉽게 알 수 있다. 영화 장면과 주인공들이 과거의 애니메이션처럼 2차원이 아니라 3차원 영상으로 만들어져서 실물과 현실에 아주 가깝다. 관객은 현실감이 뛰어나기 때문에 영화의 주인공들을 더 현실감 있게 느낀다. 또한 공중을 나는 일처럼 실제 사람이 할 수 없는 일을 그 주인공들은 할 수 있다.

현실감이 아주 뛰어나서 인간 또는 인간에 가까운 주인공들이 현실에선 불가능한 일들을 하는 좋은 예는 2009년의 아바타이다. 그 영화의 주인공들과 그들의 행성들 모두 컴퓨터로 제작되었다. 이 영화만을 위해 만들어진 주인공들만의 언어가 있을 정도이다.

컴퓨터 제작 영상 기술은 나날이 반전하므로 이 분야의 전망이 밝다. 영상 주인공들은 더욱 더 실제 인간 같고 영상의 배경 장소들은 갈수록 우리를 놀랍게 만든다. 많은 사람들은 미래에 컴퓨터 영상이 실제 배우들을 대체할 것이라고 생각한다. 어떤 면에서는 CGI배우들이 실제 배우들 보다 더 나은 점이 있다. 실제 배우들과는 달리 병에 걸리지도 않고, 촬영에 늦지 않고, 지치지 않고, 그리고 출연료를 요구하지도 않는다.

QUESTIONS FOR DISCUSSION

1. 여러분은 애니메이션 영화를 좋아하나요?
2. 여러분은 손으로 그려진 애니메이션 영화와 CGI 영화 중에서 어떤 것을 선호하나요? 선호하는 이유는?
3. 여러분은 Playstaion 또는 X-Box를 가지고 있나요? 그런 컴퓨터 게임이 컴퓨터 영상 기술이 없어도 그렇게 재미있을까요? 왜 그렇거나 그렇지 않나요?
4. 여러분은 미래에 컴퓨터 영상 배우가 실제 배우를 대체할 것이라고 생각하나요? 왜 그렇거나 그렇지 않나요?
5. 컴퓨터 영상배우만으로 영화를 제작하면 좋은 점은 어떤 것들이 있나요?
6. 실제 영화배우가 출연하는 영화를 제작할 때 부딪히는 문제점들은 (컴퓨터 영상배우들은 일으키지 않는)?
7. 만약 모든 영화가 CGI로 만들어 진다면 …
   a. 여러분은 영화를 보고싶을까요?
   b. CGI 영화가 실제 영화배우가 출연하는 영화 보다 더 흥미진진할 것이다.
   c. 만약 CGI 영화가 슬픈 내용이면 여러분은 슬퍼서 울까요?
8. 아바타 영화에서는 등장인물들을 위해 새로운 언어가 만들어졌다. 새로운 언어를 만드는데 시간이 얼마나 걸릴까, 왜 영화 제작진이 단지 이 영화만을 위해 그렇게 했을까?

9. CGI 없이 만들어진 영화와 반지의 제왕 또는 해리포터 처럼 CGI 로 만들어진 영화 중에서 어떤 액션 영화를 선호하나요? 그 이유는?
10. 지금부터 100년 후에도 영화가 존재할까요? 아니면 그 인기가 서서히 사라질까요?

29. SPACE EXPLORATION

우주항공 프로그램

한국의 우주항공연구원 (KARI) 은 한국을 2015년 까지 세계 10대 우주항공의 선두주자로 만들려고 노력한다. 대부분의 한국사람들은 한국에 우주항공 프로그램이 있다는 것 조차 모르고 있다.

한국엔 1987년에 시작된 우주항공 프로그램이 있다. 이제 한국은 세계 10대 우주항공 국가의 대열에 가까워지고 있다. 우주항공연구원은 1992년에 첫번째 시험위성을 띄웠다. 3년후에는 Koreaset One 이라는 통신위성을 띄웠다. 한국은 세계에서 23번째 상업위성을 가진 나라가 되었다.

우주항공 센터 (위성/우주선 발사 센터) 가 없이 그 어떤 나라도 우주항공 선진국이 될 수 없다. 그래서 KARI는 2008년 전남에 Naro 우주항공 센터를 세웠다. 그 비용은 2,650억원이 들었다.

Naro 우주항공 센터를 열었을 때 한국은 세계에서 13번째로 로켓을 우주로 쏘아올릴 수 있는 발사장을 가진 나라가 되었다. Naro 센터가 생기기 전에는 KARI 는 위성을 궤도에 띄우기 위해 외국의 발사장을 사용하였다. 그러나 그 비용은 아주 컸다. Naro를 세우는 비용보다도 더 많은 비용이 들었다.

모든 한국 사람들이 우주항공 프로그램에 만족스러워 하진 않는다. 어떤 사람들은 그건 많은 돈의 낭비라고 생각한다. 로켓과 발사장을 만드는 재원을 도로와 같은 국가 기간시설을 발전시키는데 사용한는 것이 더 가치가 있다고 말한다.

불행해도, 한국의 날씨는 우주 센터를 운영하기에 이상적이지 않다. 기온이 춥거나 날씨가 나쁘면 로켓을 발사할 수가 없다. 그러나 한국의 날씨는 춥거나 나쁜 경우가 많다.

QUESTIONS FOR DISCUSSION

1. 한국이 우주항공 프로그램을 갖는 것이 중요한가요? 왜 그렇거나 그렇지 않나요?
2. 전 세계 모든 나라가 우주항공 프로그램을 갖는 것이 중요한가요? 왜 그렇거나 그렇지 않나요?
3. 한국이 2015년까지 세계 10대 우주항공의 선두주자가 되거나 되지 못한는 것이 중요한가요? 왜 그렇거나 그렇지 않나요?
4. 한국이 우주항공 프로그램에 뛰어드는 것을 어떻게 생각하나요?
   a. 아주 좋은 일이다. b. 별 관심이 없다. c. 돈 낭비다. 한국은 다른 더 중요한 것에 돈을 써야 한다.
5. 어떤 사람들이 우주 비행사가 되나요? 어떤 (전문적) 기술/지식이 있어야 하나요?
6. 여러분은 우주 비행사가 되고 싶나요? 왜 그렇거나 그렇지 않나요?
7. 우주 비행사는 모두 남자여야 하나요 아니면 여자도 우주 비행사가 될 수 있나요? 왜 그렇게 생각하나요.
8. 무엇이 한국 우주항공 프로그램의 목적이어야 한다고 생각하나요? 왜 그렇게 생각하나요.
   a. 한국에서 사용되는 통신위성을 위성궤도에 띄우기.
   b. 위성을 생산하여 외국에 수출하기.
   c. 한국의 우주 비행사들을 달과 다른 행성에 보내기.

9. 한국도 미국처럼 우주왕복선을 만들어야 한다고 생각하나요? 왜 그렇거나 그렇지 않나요?
10. 기온이 춥거나 날씨가 나쁘면 로켓을 발사할 수가 없다. 그렇다면, 한국의 우주항공 프로그램은 중단되어야 하나요? 왜 그렇거나 그렇지 않나요?

30. COMPUTER LEARNING

소프트웨어

요즈음 많은 고등학교 학생들은 컴퓨터를 사용하고 있다. 이런 영리한 아이들은 21세기에 개인의 성공기회는 아마도 그의 컴퓨터 사용능력이 좌우할지도 모른다는 것을 알고 있다.

어렸을 때부터 사용 시작. 많은 현재의 고등학생들은 초등학교 때부터 컴퓨터를 사용하기 시작했다. 그 시기엔 거의 대부분의 컴퓨터 프로그램이 게임이었다. 하지만 지금은 초등학교에서 고등학교까지 모든 연령의 학생들을 위한 CD롬 교육용 소프트웨어가 많이 있다.

오늘날엔 수학, 과학, 영어, 그리고 많은 다른 과목들을 위한 학습 프로그램들이 있다. 심지어는 아직 글을 읽을 줄 모르는 걸음마를 배우는 아이들과 유치원 이전의 아이들을 위한 프로그램들도 있다.

이러한 학습 프로그램들이 과거 어느 때보다 더 쉽게 배울 수 있도록 해준다. 그리고 대부분의 아이들이 컴퓨터를 가지고 놀기를 좋아하므로, 이것이야말로 하나의 즐거운 학습방법이다. 책보다 컴퓨터를 가지고 공부하는 것이 훨씬 재미있다.

요즈음 상점에서 팔리고 있는 컴퓨터들은 멀티미디어 컴퓨터이다. 이것은 컴퓨터가 음향을 들려주고 동화상을 보여 준다는 것을 의미한다. 그리하여 오늘날의 컴퓨터는 책이라기 보다는 선생님과 같다. 그 결과는 학생들이 컴퓨터를 사용해 공부할 때 더 잘 그리고 빠르게 배운다.

그러나 책은 컴퓨터에 비해 한가지 이점이 있다. 만약 학교가는 길에 공부하고 싶으면, 지하철 또는 버스를 타고 학교에 갈 때 책을 가지고 다닐 수 있다. 물론, 노트북 컴퓨터가 있지만 비싸고 쉽게 고장난다. 또한 가지고 다니기에 무겁다.

QUESTIONS FOR DISCUSSION

1. 여러분은 컴퓨터를 가지고 있나요? 그렇다면, 다음에 답하세요.
   a. 얼마나 오랫 동안 가져 왔나요?
   b. 어떤 용도로 사용하나요? 컴퓨터로 무엇을 하나요?
   c. 여러분 또는 부모님 중에 누가 컴퓨터 구입을 결정했나요?
2. 21세기에 컴퓨터 사용이 필수적이라고 생각하나요? 왜 그렇게 생각하나요?
3. 아래의 직업들 중 어떤 직업이 21세기에 컴퓨터를 사용할 줄 아는 것을 가장 필요로 하나요? (하나 이상 선택하세요). 왜 그렇게 생각하나요.
   a. 교사 b. 의사 c. 판매원 d. 과학자 e. 비행기 조종사 f. 가게 점원 g. 비서
   h. 경찰 i. 음악가
4. 여러분은 학습용 프로그램 (소프트웨어) 이 있나요? 만약 그렇다면, 어떤 종류?
5. 컴퓨터를 사용할 줄 모르는 사람에 대해서 어떻게 생각하나요? 게으른 가요 아니면 우둔한가요? 왜 그렇게 생각하나요.

6. 책보다 컴퓨터를 가지고 공부하는 것이 훨씬 재미있다는 것에 동의하나요? 왜 그렇거나 그렇지 않나요?
7. 여러분은 사람들이 몇 살때 컴퓨터를 배우기 시작해야 한다고 생각하나요? 왜 그렇게 생각하나요?
8. 여러분은 교육용 소프트웨어가 언젠가 책과 선생님을 대체할 것이라고 생각하나요? 왜 그렇거나 그렇지 않나요?
9. 다음중 어떤 과목이 컴퓨터를 통해 배우는 것이 적합하거나 그렇지 않다고 생각하나요?
   a. 외국어 b. 수학 c. 과학 d. 역사 e. 요리 f. 음악 g. 읽기 h. 지리 i. 성교육

31. THE INTERNET

빠른 인터넷

대부분의 아이들은 인터넷을 사용하지만 그것이 새로운 기술이라는 것을 인식하지 못한다. 인터넷은 1990년대 중반부터 존재하기 시작했다. 그 당시엔 월드 와이드 웹이라고 불리었다.

느린 속도. 2000년 이전에는 인터넷을 사용하기가 힘들었다. 왜냐면 아주 느리고 사용하기 전에 항상 로그인 (sign in) 을 해야 했다. 전화선으로 연결된 모뎀을 통해서 인터넷에 연결했다. 그 모뎀을 통해 ISP (인터넷 서비스 회사) 에 전화를 걸어 연결되고 로그인을 해야했다.

그러나 점점 더 많은 사람들이 ISP의 서버를 사용함에 따라 속도는 점점 느려졌다. 어떤 경우엔 웹페이지 하나를 다운받는데 45초나 걸렸다. 브로드밴드가 일반화되기 전까지는 인터넷 사용은 짜증스러운 경험이었다.

속도가 너무 느려서 멀티미디어의 사용은 불가능했다. 음악을 듣고 동영상을 보는 것은 불가능한 일이었다. 현재 우리가 인터넷에서 할 수 있는 것들 중 거의 대부분이 2000년에는 불가능했다.

2006년이 되어서는 인터넷을 통해 음악을 다운받으며 듣고 텔레비젼을 보고 Skype 으로 화상통화를 할 수 있었다. 브로드밴드가 그 모든 것을 가능하게 해주었다.

1999년 이후 인터넷은 많이 발전했으나 또한 많이 복잡해지고 위험해졌다. 인터넷이 단순했을 때에는 바이러스를 차단하는 보호가 필요없었다. 인터넷 쇼핑 (online shopping) 이전에는 해커들이 신용카드를 훔칠 수 없었다. 이젠 그 둘 모두를 걱정해야 한다.

QUESTIONS FOR DISCUSSION

1. 여러분은 인터넷을 사용하나요? 그렇다면, 다음 질문에 답하세요.
   a. 얼마나 오랫 동안 사용했나요?
   b. 어떤 용도로 사용하나요? 인터넷에서 무엇을 하나요?
   c. 어디에서 사용 방법을 배웠나요? 누가 가르쳐 주었나요?
2. 전자우편과 일반우편 중 어느 것을 선호하나요? 그 이유는?
3. 영어를 아는 것이 인터넷 사용에 중요한가요 아니면 한글만 알아도 되나요? 왜 그렇거나 그렇지 않나요?
4. 여러분은 컴퓨터 바이러스로부터 컴퓨터를 어떻게 보호하나요?
5. 신용카드 정보를 훔치는 해커들은 어떤 처벌을 받아야 마땅할까요? 왜 그렇게 생각하나요?
6. 여러분이 아주 어렸을 때와 비교했을 때 인터넷은 얼마나 많이 변했나요? 10년 전에는 불가능했으나 지금은 할 수 있는 것들은?
7. 어린 아이들이 몇 살때 컴퓨터를 배우기 시작해야 한다고 생각하나요? 왜 그렇게 생각하나요?

8. 아이들이 인터넷 사용을 배우는 것이 얼마나 중요하다고 생각하나요? 왜 그렇게 생각하나요?
   a. 아주 중요하다.   b. 약간 중요하다.   c. 인터넷을 배울 필요가 없다.
9. 고등학교 학생이 인터넷을 사용할 줄 아는 것이 얼마나 중요한가요? 인터넷 사용법을 몰라도 좋은 직업을 구할 수 있을까요? 그렇다면, 어떤 직업?
10. 여러분은 인터넷이 없은 세상에서 살고 싶나요? 왜 그렇거나 그렇지 않나요?

32. FASHION AWARENESS

사치품 세대

한국의 젊은이들이 친구들과 시간을 보내기 좋아하는 서울의 압구정동, 청담동에는 프라다, 구찌, 그리고 루이브통 같은 디자이너 전문점으로 가득차 있다. 오늘날 한국 대학생들의 66퍼센트가 디자이너 상품 (명품) 을 가지고 있다.

이전에는 그러한 디자이너 상품을 사는 사람들의 대부분은 삼십대 이상이었으나, 현재는 더 젊은 사람들이 산다. 디자이너 상표를 사는 20대가 증가하는 반면30대의 비율은 줄어들고 있다.

신용카드 빚. 이러한 디자이너 상표에 대한 욕구는 한국의 젊은이들에게 많은 문제를 일으키고 있다. 그들은 돈이 충분히 없기 때문에 신용카드를 사용한다. 그 결과 아주 많은 신용카드 빚을 지게 되고 갚지 못하게 된다.

왜 젊은이들은 갚을 능력도 없으면서 그런 비싼 물건을 사는 것일까? 왜냐하면 친구들이 모두 명품을 가지고 있어서 그들 또한 똑같은 것들을 갖고 싶기 때문이다.

믿기 힘든 일이지만 일부 부모님들은 자녀들에게 그런 사치품들을 사준다. 그런 아이들을 사치품 세대라 부른다. 디자이너 상품을 사는 주된 이유는 자랑하기 위해서이다. 친구들이 그들을 부유하다고 생각하길 원한다.

일부 직장이 있는 젊은이들은 친구들로부터 부러움을 사기 (좋은 인상을 주기) 위해 명품을 사는데 월급 전체를 쓰기도 한다. 중고 유럽명품을 파는 인터넷 웹사이트도 많이 있다. 그런 중고명품을 사는 사람들은 한국에서 판매되는 새 명품을 살 형편이 안되는 사람들이다.

디자이너 상품중엔 매우 비싼 것들도 있다. 여자 손지갑이 인터넷에서 2백5십만원까지 하는 것도 있다. 그것을 전문점에서 사면 심지어 더 비싸다.

QUESTIONS FOR DISCUSSION

1. 디자이너 상품을 사는데 모든 돈을 사용하는 사람들에 대해서 어떻게 생각하나요? 왜 그렇게 생각하나요.
   a. 그들은 패션의 유행을 안다.   b. 그들은 바보스럽다.
2. 청바지를 어디에서 사고싶나요? 그 이유는?
   a. 시장에서 (만원)   b. 할인매장에서 (만오천원)   c. 백화점 (십만원)
3. 만약 여러분이 아주 부유하다면, 청바지를 어디에서 살까요? 그 이유는?
   a. 시장에서   b. 할인매장에서   c. 백화점
4. 비싼 옷을 입은 사람을 보면 여러분도 똑같은 옷을 갖고 싶나요? 왜 그렇거나 그렇지 않나요?
5. 왜 많은 한국 사람들이 비싼 차와 디자이너 옷을 소유하고 싶어하나요? 왜 그렇게 생각하나요.
   a. 다른 사람들의 부러움을 사기 위해
   b. 인생에 성공한 것처럼 느끼고 싶어서
   c. 그들이 어렸을 때 가난했기 때문에

6. 여러분은 어떤 것이 돈을 가장 잘 쓰는 방법이라고 생각하나요? 이유는?
   a. 다 쓴다　b. 저축한다　c. 가난한 사람들에게 준다
7. 여러분은 옷을 자주 사나요? 그렇다면, 얼마나 자주 어디에서 사나요?
8. 여러분은 돈 쓰는 것을 즐기나요? 왜 그렇거나 그렇지 않나요?

33. CARS AND DRIVING

안전 운전

한국에서 십대에 면허증을 갖는 것은 평범한 일이 아니지만 미국이나 뉴질랜드 같은 나라에서는 대부분 고등학교 다닐때 면허증을 취득한다. 그런 나라에서는 14 또는 15세가 운전을 할 수 있는 나이이다.

고등학교에는 운전교육 과목이 있다. 그리고 모든 학생들 – 남학생, 여학생 모두 – 그 수업을 받는다. 그 수업을 받는 동안 학생들은 단지 차를 운전하는 것만 배우는 것이 아니라 안전하게 운전하는 법을 배운다.

운전을 잘 한다는 것은 단지 차의 조정장치들을 잘 다루는 것 이상을 의미한다. 그건 또한 다른 운전자들을 고려하고 때로는 양보를 해야한다는 것을 의미한다. 또한 안전속도로 운전을 하고 교통법규를 지켜야 한다는 것을 의미한다.

위험한 운전. 핸드폰이 위험한 운전의 새로운 원인으로 추가되었다. 운전하면서 전화를 하고 텍스트 메세지를 보내다가 아주 많은 교통사고를 일으킨다. 전화하며 운전하는 사람들은 운전보다는 전화통화에 집중한다.

그 결과, 그들은 때때로 빨간 신호등을 통과하거나 정지선에서 서지 않기도 한다. 그들은 평상시에는 절대로 일부러 그렇게 하진 않을 것이다.

시끄러운 음악. 젊은 운전자들은 때때로 CD나 MP3를 아주 시끄럽게 켜고 들으며 운전하다. 시끄러운 음악은 운전을 방해해서 그들이 운전하고 있다는 사실을 잊게 만든다. 그런 음악은 또한 다른 운전자들을 방해한다. 다른 한가지 운전하면서 하지 말아야 할 것은 음식을 먹는 것이다. 때로는 운전하며 먹거나 마시는 운전자들에 의해 교통사고가 일어난다.

QUESTIONS FOR DISCUSSION

1. 여러분은 운전면허증이 있나요? 만약 없다면, 갖고 싶나요? 만약 그렇다면, 그 이유는?
2. 한국에서 운전면허를 딸 수 있는 최소 연령은? 그것에 동의하나요 아니면 낮춰져야 한다고 생각하나요? 그렇다면, 그 이유는?
3. 한국의 도로에는 차가 많다. 차의 수를 줄이기 위한 다음의 제안사항 중 어떤 것에 동의하나요? 왜 그렇거나 그렇지 않나요?
   a. 운전면허 최소연령을 21세로 높인다.
   b. 현재보다 운전면허 시험을 아주 힘들게 만든다.
   c. 가족당 2명만이 운전 면허증을 가질수 있는 제한을 둔다.
4. 대부분의 한국 운전자들은 교통법규를 잘 지키나요? 왜 그렇게 생각하나요?
   a. 그렇다, 대부분 잘 지킨다.　b. 아니다, 그렇지 않다. 많은 운전자들이 교통법규를 무시한다.
5. 운전중에 핸드폰을 사용하는 운전자들은 체포되어야 (단속되어야) 하나요? 만약 아니라면, 그들이 어떤 처벌을 받아야 하지 않나요? 그렇다면, 어떤 처벌?

6. 음주운전을 하다가 교통사로를 유발하는 운전자들은 어떤 처벌을 받아야 하나요?
7. 여성 운전자들에 대한 여러분의 의견은? 남성들보다 운전을 못하거나, 비슷하거나, 아니면 더 잘 하나요? 왜 그렇게 생각하나요.
8. 왜 자동차 보험이 젊은 운전자들 보다 나이 많은 운전자들에게 더 저렴한가요? 왜 젊은 운전자들의 보험이 더 비싼가요?
9. 다음과 같은 일을 하는 운전자들은 어떤 처벌을 받아야 하나요? 벌금? 감옥? 그렇다면, 얼마의 금액 또는 기간?
   a. 빨간 신호등 통과하기 (무시하기)
   b. 정지선 통과하기
   c. 음주운전
   d. 핸드폰으로 통화하기

34. UFOs AND CIRCLES

미확인 비행물체 미스테리

누구나 UFO는 미확인 비행물체의 약자라는 것을 알고 있다. 그렇지만UFO는 진짜 있나요? 그렇다면 어디에서 왔고 무엇을 얻고자 왜 지구에 왔을까?

UFO에 대한 이론은 여러개가 있다. 일부 사람들은 UFO가 외계인이 탑승한 우주선이라고 생각한다. UFO에 대해 회의적인 (믿지 않는) 사람들은 UFO나 외계인을 보았다고 보고하는 사람들은 거짓말을 하거나 미쳤다고 생각한다.

그러나 UFO가 실제로 존재한다고 믿는 사람들의 숫자가 늘고 있다. 왜냐면 너무 많은 UFO 보고 자료 (증거물) 들을 논리적으로 설명할 수 없기 때문이다. 전 세계에서 목격된 UFO의 놀라운 사진들이 분석되었다. 그중 일부는 한국에서 목격되었다, 그리고 많은 경우는 비디오로 촬영되었다.

Crop Circles. 외계인들이 우리가 볼 수 있는 표시를 지상에 남기고 있다는 것이 가능한 일인가? 그런 사인은 Crop Circle 이라 불리는데 매우 아름답고 복잡하다. 그런 Crop Circle 은 밀이나 보리밭에 만들어 진다.

그런 곡물밭에 만들어지는 문양들의 일부는 인간이 만든 것임을 안다. 하지만 다른 문양들은 인간이 만들기엔 그 규모가 너무 크고 복잡하고 완벽하다. 어떤 경우에는 몇 분만에 만들어 진다. 인간은 그런 기술이 없다.

위에 보이는 문양을 보면, 각각 숫자를 표시하는 13개의 상징이 있다. 모든 가로 세로 그리고 대각선을 더하면 369가 된다. 그 상징들은 옆의 챠트처럼 정렬되어 있다. 각각 다른 색깔은 다른 상징을 의미한다. 모든 보라색을 더하면 369가 된다. 이런 챠트를 디자인 할 정도로 똑똑한 인간이 있을까? 그렇다면, 그런 똑똑한 사람이 곡물밭에 나가 문양을 만들고 있을까?

QUESTIONS FOR DISCUSSION

1. UFO는 무엇이라고 생각하나요? 왜 그렇게 생각하나요.
   a. 지구상을 비행하는 외계인이다. b. 비행기나 헬리콥터를 타고 날아다니는 사람들이다.
   c. 차 불빛이거나 지구상에 존재하는 다른 불빛이다.
2. UFO를 본 적이 있나요? 그렇다면, 그 경험을 이야기 해 보세요. 그렇지 않다면, UFO를 보고싶나요? 왜 그렇거나 그렇지 않나요?
3. 만약 실제로 외계인을 보았다면 대부분의 사람들은 어떻게 할까요? 왜 그렇게 생각하나요.
   a. 직접 만나려고 노력한다. b. 공포에 질려 도망갈 것이다. c. 외계인을 죽이려 할 것이다.

4. 이런 문양을 디자인 할 정도로 똑똑한 사람이 있나요? 그렇다면, 디자인 하는데 얼마나 오래 걸리고, 그런 똑똑한 사람이 밤에, 때로는 비가오는 날에, 곡물밭에 나가 문양을 만들고 있을까요?
5. 왜 그 누가 실제로 본적도 없으면서 UFO를 보았다고 거짓말을 할까요? 여러분은 그 사람들이 거짓말을 하거나 미쳤다고 생각하나요?
6. 만약 외계인들이 곡물밭에 문양을 만들고 있다면 왜 만든다고 생각하나요? 그들이 우리에게 무언가를 말하려고 하는 건가요? 그렇다면, 무엇을?
7. 일부 곡물 문양은 사람들에 의해 만들어졌다. 왜 그 사람들이 그것을 만들었을까?
8. 만약 UFO와 Crop Circles 이 실제라면, 왜 외계인이 지구상에 있을까? 그들은 무엇을 원하는가? 그들은 친절할까 아니면 그렇지 않을까? 왜 그렇게 생각하나요?
9. 만약 UFO와 Crop Circles 이 실제라면, 왜 외계인들은 지상에 표시만을 남기는 대신 우리와 대화하려는 노력을 하지 않을까?
10. 대부분의 영화를 보면 외계인들은 인간을 해치려하는 악한 대상이다. 여러분은 그것이 외계인들을 표현하는 (영상에서 보여주는) 좋은 방법이라고 생각하나요?

35. DINOSAURS

공룡이 지구에 존재했을때

1990년도에 가장 인기 있었던 영화는 쥬리기 공원과 그 영화 후편 2개였다. 세개의 영화 모두 박스 오프스의 흥행작이었다.

왜 공룡에 관한 영화가 그렇게 인기가 있을까요? 왜냐하면 전 세계에 걸쳐 젊은 사람들과 나이든 사람들 모두 공룡에 매료되기 때문이다. 그 이유는 공룡이 거대하고 또한 1억 5천만년전에 지구를 지배했기 때문이다.

공룡은 지구에 존재했던 가장 큰 동물이다. 공룡들 중에 브론커사우루스는 10미터 높이, 25미터 길이 그리고 몸무게가 10톤에 달했다. 그러나 공룡학자들은 여전히 공룡에 대해 배우고 있다. 1985년에 발견된 공룡은 54미터 길이에 2억 2천5만년전에 살던 동물이었다. 그것은 존재했던 공룡들 중에 가장 큰 동물이었기 때문에 수퍼사우르스라고 이름이 붙여졌다.

1817년 이전에는 공룡이 존재했다는 것을 아는 사람은 아무도 없었다. 그해에 윌리엄 버클랜드라는 영국의 과학자가 거대한 동물의 이빨을 발견했다. 과학자들은 충격에 휩싸였다. 그들은 지구상에 그렇게 큰 동물이 존재했다는 것을 알지 못했다.

1850년에 거대한 이빨과 뼈가 발견되고 공룡이라는 이름이 탄생했다. 우리는 이제 공룡이 지구상에 존재했던 가장 큰 동물이라는 것과 언제 공룡이 존재했는지도 알고 있다. 공룡은 인간이 지구를 지배했던 것보다 더 오랫동안 지구를 지배했다. 아래 도표는 공룡이 살았던 1억 5천년과 인간이 살기 시작한 10만년전을 비교했다.

이 도표 비교에서 인간은 지구상에 방금 도착했다 (아주 짧은 시간 살고 있다). 더 이상 쥬리기 공원의 영화에서처럼 큰 공룡들이 살고 있지 않지만 새들과 같은 그들은 후손들은 여전히 살고 있다.

QUESTIONS FOR DISCUSSION

1. 여러분도 공룡에 매료되나요? 여러분들도 어렸을때 공룡에 심취했나요?
2. 쥬리기 공원 영화를 보았나요? 그 영화를 좋아했나요? 그렇다면 왜 그렇게 생각하는지 말하세요.

3. 사람들이 공룡이 세상에서 존재하지 않아도 공룡에 관심을 갖는 이유는 무엇일까요? 왜 그렇게 생각하는지 말하세요.
4. 만약 공룡을 다시 살릴 수 있다면 그것은 좋은 생각일까요? 왜 그렇게 생각하는지 말하세요.
   a. 예, 다시 살려 내자.　　b. 채식동물만 살려 내고 육식동물은 살려내선 안된다.
   c. 아니오, 어떤 공룡도 다시 살려내서는 안된다.
5. 만약 공룡이 오늘날 우리 지구에 산다면 우리가 공룡을 지배할 수 있을까요? 왜 그렇게 생각하는지 말하세요.
   a. 그렇다, 우리는 공룡을 지배할 수 있을 것이다.　　b. 작은 공룡들만 지배할 수 있을 것이다.
   c. 아니다, 공룡들이 우리를 잡아먹을 것이다.
6. 만약 쥬라기 공원이 실제라면, 여러분은 공룡을 보기 위해 가고 싶을까요? 왜 그런지 그렇지 않은지 말하세요.
7. 만약 오늘날 공룡이 산다면 어디에 살까요? 공룡들을 같은 장소에 계속 머물게 하는것이 가능할까요? 왜 그런지 그렇지 않은지 말하세요.
8. 어떤 사람들은 모든 동물들은 동물원이 아닌 야생에서 살아야 한다고 생각한다. 그것에 대해 어떻게 생각하나요? 왜 그렇게 생각하는지 말하세요.
9. 공룡은 1억 5천년동안 지구에 살았다. 인간도 또한 그렇게 오래 지구를 지배할까요?

36. ANIMALS AND PETS

애완견

요즘에 점점 더 많은 한국인들이 애완동물을 키우고 있다. 많은 사람들이 다른 어떤 종류의 동물보다 개를 애완동물로 키우고 있다. 왜냐하면 한국의 수퍼마켓이나 할인마트에서 다른 어떤 종류의 동물보다 개를 위한 장난감과 애완동물 식품을 많이 판매하기 때문이다.

개는 사랑스럽고 주인에게 충성하기 때문에 집에서 기를 수 있는 좋은 애완동물이다. 또한 개는 날카로운 이빨과 큰소리로 짖는 것 때문에 도둑을 위협 할 수 있다. 그러나 많은 사람들이 개를 무서워하기 때문에 친구들도 위협할 수 있다.

우리는 밖에서 줄에 묶여져서 자유롭게 돌아다닐 수 없는 개들을 종종 본다. 그들의 주인들은 단지 집에 도둑이 들어오지 못하게 하기 위한 목적으로 개를 기른다. 그러나 개들은 많은 운동이 필요하다. 항상 개를 묶어놓는 것은 개한테 힘든 일이다.

개와 고양이

그러나 개만 좋은 애완동물이 되는 것은 아니다. 고양이와 새들 또한 좋은 친구가 될 수 있다. 그 동물들은 사랑스러울 뿐만 아니라 개보다 대체로 조용하다.

고양이는 매우 깨끗한 동물이다. 고양이는 거의 계속적으로 그들의 혀로 자신을 몸을 닦는다. 몸이 깨끗하기 때문에 털에서 좋은 냄새가 난다. 개들은 스스로 몸을 닦지 않기 때문에 목욕을 시켜 주어야 한다. 만약 개들이 목욕을 하지 않으면 냄새가 난다.

고양이는 밖에서 산책을 할 필요가 없지만 개는 산책이 필요하다. 개들은 하루에 2~3번은 밖에 데리고 나가야 한다. 고양이는 Litter박스라고 불리는 집안에 있는 화장실을 사용한다. 개는 그렇게 화장실을 사용하는 것을 모른다.

새들 또한 좋은 애완동물이 될 수 있다. 새들은 사람들이 생각하는 것보다 더 똑똑하며 어떤 새들은 심지어 말을 할 수 있다. 그러나 애완조는 날개 끝부분의 깃털을 잘라야 한다. 그렇지 않으면, 언제가는 열린 창문이나 문을 통해 날아갈 수 있다.

QUESTIONS FOR DISCUSSION

1. 여러분은 애완동물이 있나요? 그렇다면, 어떤 종류의 애완동물이며 언제부터 길렀나요?
2. 모든 사람들이 애완동물이 있어야 하나요? 왜 그런지 그렇지 않은지 말하세요.
3. 어떤 종류의 동물이 가장 좋은 애완동물이 된다고 생각하나요? 왜 그렇게 생각하는지 말하세요.
4. 물고기가 좋은 애완동물인가요? 왜 그런지 그렇지 않은지 말하세요.
5. 어떤 사람들은 뱀, 사자, 상어 같은 위험한 동물을 애완동물로 기르고 있다. 다음 사항에서 어떤 의견에 동의하는지 또한 왜 동의하는지 말하세요.
   a. 위험한 동물들은 절대 애완동물로 키워서는 안된다.
   b. 야생에서 자라지 않았다면 위험한 동물들을 갖는 것은 괜찮다.
   c. 어린 위험한 동물들은 괜찮지만 큰 위험한 동물들은 안된다.
6. 애완동물을 가지고 있는 사람들은 동물을 싫어하는 사람들과 다른가요? 그렇다면, 어떻게 다른가요?
7. 어떤 사람들은 자신의 아기처럼 애완동물을 다룬다. 그들은 옷을 사주고 털을 다른 색깔로 염색을 해준다. 그것에 대해 어떻게 생각하나요? 여러분도 그렇게 하고 싶나요? 왜 그런지, 그렇지 않은지 말하세요.
8. 애완동물이 있는 노인들이 애완동물이 없는 노인들보다 더 오래 산다. 그렇게 되는 이유는 무엇일까요?
9. 개는 매우 영리한 동물이지만 어떤 한국 사람들은 식용으로 먹는 것을 좋아한다. 여러분은 영리한 동물들을 먹는건 괜찮다고 생각하나요? 왜 그런지 그렇지 않은지 말하세요.
   a. 영리하지 않은 멍청한 동물들을 먹는 것은 괜찮다.
   b. 어떤 동물이든 먹는건 괜찮다. 모든 동물들은 먹기 위한 것이다.
   c. 사람은 동물을 전혀 먹어서는 안된다. 먹어서 안되는 이유는?
10. 어떤 사람들은 고기를 전혀 먹지 않는다. 그런 사람들은 채식주의자라고 불린다. 인간이 채소로만 건강 할 수 있나요?

37. PROFESSIONAL SPORTS

프로 스포츠는 한국에서 매우 인기가 높다. 축구팀, 야구팀 그리고 농구팀이 있다. 이 팀들은 전국의 여러 도시에 각각 연고를 두고 있다. 대부분의 사람들은 자신의 고향팀을 응원한다.

야구경기는 1800년대초에 북미에서 창안되었고 최초 미국팀들은 1850년대에 결성되었다. 미국에서 야구는 “전국민이 즐기는 오락” 이라고 불릴만큼 인기가 높다.

북미 이외에 유일하게 프로 야구팀이 있는 나라는 일본과 한국이다. 미국 선교사들이 1904년에 야구게임을 한국에 전파했다.

한국 최초의 야구팀은 1905년에 창설된 어느 고등학교팀이었다. 한국의 프로야구 리그는 1982년에 조직되었고 현재 전국에 8개의 팀이 있다.

미국에서와 같이 한국의 야구팬들은 자신의 팀을 응원하고 야구경기에 열광한다. 한국팀들은 각 팀마다 응원

단까지 있다.

야구는 단체경기 중 하나이다. 이것은 여러명의 선수들이 함께 팀을 이뤄 경기를 하는 것을 말한다. 또 다른 단체경기로는 축구, 배구, 농구, 하키등이 있다.

다른 팀스포츠와 마찬가지로 야구의 경우 경기의 승패를 결정하는 두가지 주요인은 다음과 같다. 1) 각 선수가 얼마나 잘 하느냐. 2) 모든 선수들이 얼마나 잘 호흡을 맞추느냐.

아주 뛰어난 선수들은 대부분 유명해진다. 때때로 한국 선수들이 미국에 있는 야구팀에 들어간다. 그러한 선수들은 항상 미국과 한국 모두에서 스타가 된다. 그것은 수퍼 스타가 되기 위한 모든 프로 선수들의 꿈이다.

QUESTIONS FOR DISCUSSION

1. 좋아하는 스포츠가 있나요? 그렇다면 무엇인지, 그리고 직접 경기를 하는지 아니면 보기만 하나요?
2. 여러분은 프로 야구의 팬이세요? 그렇다면 가장 좋아하는 팀은 무엇인가요?
3. 프로 야구경기에 직접 가본적이 있나요? 경기장에서 경기를 보는것과 텔레비젼으로 경기를 보는것 중 어떤 것을 더 좋아하나요?
4. 어떤 나라에서는 유명한 스포츠 선수들이 어마어마한 연봉을 받는다. 그것에 대해 어떻게 생각하나요? 왜 그렇게 생각하는지 말하세요.
   a. 선수들은 거액의 연봉을 받아서는 안된다. b. 그건 문제가 되지 않는다. 더 많이 받을수록 더 좋다.
5. 여러분은 개인 스포츠 경기와 팀 스포츠 경기 중에 어떤 것을 더 선호하나요? 왜 그렇게 생각하는지 말하세요.
6. 운동 선수들이 프로팀에서 뛰는것을 더 선호하는 가장 중요한 이유는 무엇이라고 생각하나요?
   a. 왜냐하면 그들은 스포츠를 하는것을 좋아하기 때문이다.
   b. 그렇게 해서 그들은 유명해질 수가 있기 때문이다.
   c. 그렇게 해서 그들은 많은 돈을 벌 수 있기 때문이다.
7. 올림픽 경기와 프로 스포츠 경기중 어떤 스포츠를 보는 것을 더 좋아 하나요? 왜 그렇게 생각하는지 말하세요.
8. 여러분은 프로 스포츠팀에서 뛰고 싶은가요? 왜 그런지 또는 왜 그렇지 않은지 말하세요.
9. 우리의 삶에서 프로 스포츠는 얼마나 중요한가요? 왜 스포츠 경기가 중요한가요? 왜 그런지 또는 왜 그렇지 않은지 말하세요.
10. 서로 상대국을 싫어하는 나라들 사이에 스포츠가 어떻게 관계를 개선시킬 수 있나요?

38. HOBBIES

휴식시간

대부분의 고교생들은, 특히 대학에 가려고 결심한 경우, 자유시간이 거의 없다. 한국 학생들은 대학에 가기 위해 많은 시간을 입시공부와 영어회화 공부에 사용해야 한다.

그러나 누구에게나 그렇듯이 고교생들도 하는 일에서 벗어나 휴식할 수 있는 시간이 필요하다. 모든 사람들은 나이가 적든 많든, 때때로 자신의 일이나 학업에서 벗어날 수 있는 취미를 적어도 하나는 가지고 있어야 한다.

스포츠. 스포츠는 많은 십대 남학생들이 즐기는 취미이다. 친구들과 축구를 하거나, 체육관에서 바디빌딩을 하거나, 연을 날리거나 그 어떤 것이라도 학교 공부와 대학 입시 시험 공부에서 벗어나 쉴 수 있는 좋은 방법이다.

컴퓨터. 많은 남학생들과 그리고 또한 일부 여학생들은 컴퓨터를 사용하고 인터넷에 접속하는 것이 취미이다. 그것은 또한 학습에 좋은 방법이다. 그러나 인터넷은 또한 너무 재미있기 때문에 학교 공부는 소홀히 하며 너무 많은 시간을 온라인에서 보내기가 쉽다.

음악. 음악을 듣는것, 특히 팝뮤직을 듣는것은 여학생 그리고 남학생들이 좋아하는 여가이다. 대부분 학생들은 그들이 가장 좋아하는 가수들의 CD를 수집하는것을 즐긴다. 그것의 하나의 단점은 CD가 비싸다는 것이다. 그러나 이제는 인터넷을 통해 MP3 음악을 다운 받을 수 있다.

아트. 예술에 재능이 있는 십대들은 그들이 시간을 그림을 그리고 색칠을 하는데 보낸다. 이 학생들에게는 아트는 취미 이상이다. 많은 학생들은 장래를 위해 디자인이나 건축학을 준비한다.

십대들이 가질 수 있는 취미들은 무수히 많다. 취미는 장래의 직업을 준비할 수 있는 좋은 방법이며 게다가 마음을 편안하게 쉴 수 있는 방법이기도 하다.

QUESTIONS FOR DISCUSSION

1. 특별한 관심사나 취미는 무엇인가요? 언제 그것에 관심을 갖게 되었으며 얼마나 자주 하나요?
2. 아래 사항중에 어떤 것에 동의 하나요 그렇다면 왜 그런가요?
   a. 예, 모든 십대들은 때때로 공부에서 벗어나기 위해 취미는 꼭 가져야 한다.
   b. 아니다, 학생들은 공부에서 벗어나면 안된다. 학생들은 공부를 열심히 해야한다, 그래서 취미를 위한 시간은 없다.
3. 방과후에 얼마나 많은 시간을 취미나 특별한 관심사에 보내야 하나요? 왜 그렇게 생각하나요?
   a. 매일 조금씩 b. 주말에만 c. 대학 입시까지는 취미를 위한 시간은 없다.
4. 학국 학생들은 어릴때부터 대부분 시간을 공부와 학원을 가는데 보낸다. 더 많은 시간을 취미를 위해 보내고 공부는 덜 해야 하나요? 왜 그런지 그렇지 않는지 말하세요.
5. 어떤 활동들이 고등학교 학생들에게 좋은가요? 어떤 것은 그렇지 않나요? 왜 그런지 그렇지 않은지 말하세요.
   a. 피아노 치기 b. 컴퓨터 게임 c. 그림 그리기 d. 축구하기 e. 바디빌딩 f. TV 시청하기
   g. 등산하기 h. 인터넷 채팅방 i. 영어 배우기
6. 사람이 공부만 하고 휴식을 취하기 않는다는 것이 가능한가요? 왜 그런지 그렇지 않은지 말하세요.
7. 모든 고등학교 학생들은 학교 클럽과 스포츠 팀에 소속되어야 하나요? 왜 그런지 그렇지 않은지 말하세요.
8. 학교 일과중의 일부분은 공부와 시험과는 관견되지 않은 다른 활동을 하는데 사용되야 하나요? 왜 그렇거나 그렇지 않나요?

39. COMPUTER GAMING

게임의 세계

한국은 컴퓨터 게임의 세계 수도이다. 전세계 인터넷 게임머들은 게임 대회를 참여하기 위해 한국에 온다.

전국에 수천개의 게임방들이 퍼져있고 대부분 게임방은 24시간 동안 운영된다. 왜냐하면 게임머들이 일단 게임을 시작하면 게임을 그만두고 집에 갈 수 없기 때문이다. 그들은 전세계 게임머들과 게임을 하기 때문에 한국은 늦은 밤에 다른 어느 곳은 아직 한낮이다.

한국이 게임머들의 천국이 될 수 있는 이유는 인터넷 속도가 매우 빠르기 때문이다. 게임머들은 굉장히 빠른

인터넷 연결 속도가 필요하며 한국이 제일 빠른 국가이다.

컴퓨터 게임의 세계는 CGI 그래픽을 사용해서 만들기 때문에 현실보다 더 생생하다. 게임머들은 매우 흥미로운 게임 속의 장소때문에 게임에 빠져들게 되고 그 게임이 현실에서 실제로 일어난다고 느낀다. 각각의 게임머들은 게임에서 자신을 대표하는 아바타를 선택한다.

대부분 십대, 특히 남학생들은 컴퓨터 게임에 관심을 갖지만, 부모들이나 선생님들은 그렇지 않다. 그들은 게임은 시간 낭비라고 생각한다.

2003년 캐나다 한 대학에서 실시된 연구에서 인터넷 게임을 한 한생들이 인터넷 게임을 하지 않는 학생들보다 시각적으로 더 정확하게 기억하고 위험한 상황에 더 빠르게 대처한다고 한다.

그러나 대부분 부모들은 아이들이 컴퓨터 게임이 아닌 시험 공부에 그들의 시간을 보내야 한다고 생각한다.

그러나 더 큰 문제는 컴퓨터 게임 중독이다. 어떤 학생들은 컴퓨터 게임에 너무 중독되어 게임하는 것을 멈출 수 가 없다.

QUESTIONS FOR DISCUSSION

1. 여러분도 게임머인가요? 컴퓨터 게임하는 것을 좋아하나요? 그렇다면, 게임의 어떤 것을 좋아하나요? 그렇지 않다면, 왜 컴퓨터 게임을 좋아하지 않나요?
2. 한국이 컴퓨터 게임의 중심이 되는 것을 어떻게 생각하나요? 왜 그렇게 생각하는지 말하세요.
   a. 좋다고 생각한다. 국가의 큰 명예이다. b. 그것은 중요하지 않다. 게임은 자랑할 만한 것이 아니다.
3. 다른나라 사람보다 한국 사람들이 더 게임하는 것은 좋아하나요? 왜 게임이 한국에서 그렇게 널리 퍼졌나요?
4. 일반적으로 말해서, 아시아인들은 서양 국가의 사람들보다 더 게임을 좋아한다. 왜 그렇다고 생각하나요?
5. 보통 남자들이 여자들보다 더 게임을 좋아한다. 왜 여자들이 남자들보다 더 게임을 좋아하지 않나요? 왜 그렇게 생각하나요?
6. 미국에서, 평균 게임머 나이는 33세이다, 그러나 게임을 사는 구매자들의 나이는 40세이다. 어떻게 그 나이 차이를 설명할 수 있나요?
7. 영국에서, 평균 게임머들의 나이는 23세이다, 그러나 미국은 33세 이다. 한국의 평균 게임머들의 나이는 얼마일까요? 왜 그렇게 생각하는지 말하세요.
8. 한국의 게임방들에 대해 어떻게 생각하나요? 그곳이 젊은이들이 놀고 어울릴 수 있는 좋은 장소인가요? 왜 그런지 그렇지 않은지 말해보세요?
9. 어떤 사람들은 게임에 중독되지만 어떤 사람들은 그렇지 않다. 어떤 사람들은 멈출 때를 알지만 어떤 사람들은 중독이 되는 이유는 무엇일까요? 왜 그렇게 생각하는지 말하세요.
10. 비디오 게임 이외에는 다른 것을 하고 싶어 하지 않는 학생들에게 가장 좋은 것은 무엇일까요? 왜 그렇게 생각하는지 말하세요.

40. RELIGION

한국의 기독교

한국에는 기도할 수 있는 장소가 많이 있다. 많은 불교사찰 이외에도 또한 수 많은 기독교 교회가 있다. 한국은 아시아에서 유일하게 기독교가 많이 전파된 국가이다.

모든 다른 아시아 국가들에서는 기독교 교회를 찾기가 쉽지 않다. 그러면 왜 한국에 수많은 기독교인들이 있을까? 무엇이 한국을 그렇게 특별하게 만들었을까?

그 이유는 1910년부터 1945년까지 35년 동안 일본이 한국을 지배했기 때문이다. 그 점령기 동안 기독교 신앙은 한국이 일본에 저항해 싸울 수 있는 수단이 되었다.

한국에서 최초의 교회는 1800년대 후반에 카톨릭 선교사들에 의해 세워졌다, 그러나 1910년 일본이 한국을 침략하기 전까지는 기독교가 널리 퍼지지는 않았다.

일제 점령기에 일본인 지배자들이 한국어의 사용을 금지했지만 기독교 그룹들은 한글로 교회 가르침을 인쇄 배포하여 한글을 연명시켰다. 그것은 또한 그들이 기독교 신앙을 한국 국민들에게 전파할 수 있는 좋은 수단이 되었다.

오늘날 카톨릭, 침례교, 감리교, 장로교 그리고 몰몬교를 포함한 많은 다른 기독교 분파가 있다. 이것들은 모두 기독교의 각각 다른 분파들이다. 각각 분파마다 풍습은 다르지만 모든 분파가 2000년 전에 인류를 구원한 예수님을 믿는다는 것은 같다.

그러나 기독교 신앙은 한국의 역사에서 매우 새로운 종교이다. 한국 역사의 뿌리는 다른 모든 아시아 국가들처럼 불교에 있다. 한국에는 아직도 기독교 교회보다 불교 사찰이 더 많이 있다.

한국에서 기독교 신앙의 역사는 150년보다 짧지만 불교 신앙은 중국에서 처음 소개된 기원후 372년까지 거슬러 올라간다.

한국의 종교에 대한 것 중 가장 흥미로운 것은 많은 기독교 교회와, 불교 사찰이 있지만 대분은 한국 사람들은 종교가 없다고 말한다는 것이다.

QUESTIONS FOR DISCUSSION

1. 여러분은 종교가 있나요? 만약에 그렇다면, 여러분의 종교는 무엇이고 어떻게 그 종교인이 되었나요?
2. 여러분은 왜 사람들이 기독교 교회에 가입한다고 생각하나요? 왜 그렇게 생각하는지 말하세요.
   a. 왜냐하면 예수님을 사랑하기 때문에.
   b. 왜냐하면 교회는 파티가 있는 사교장 같은 곳이기 때문에.
   c. 왜냐하면 예수님이 그들의 문제해결을 도와주길 원해서.
3. 성인들은 교회나 다른 종교의 일원이 되어야 하나요? 왜 그렇거나 그렇지 않나요?
4. 교회를 다니는 아이들이 교회를 다니지 않는 아이들보다 더 좋은 학생들인가요? 왜 그렇게 생각하는지 말하세요.
5. 교회를 다니는 사람들이 교회를 다니지 않는 사람보다 더 정직하고 친절한가요? 왜 그렇게 생각하는지 말하세요.
6. 기독교인들이 불교인들보다 더 신앙적인가요, 아니면 둘다 같은가요? 왜 그렇게 생각하는지 말하세요.
7. 대부분 한국 사람들은 종교가 없다고 말한다. 왜 한국인들이 95% 이상이 불교인인 동남 아시아 사람들보다 덜 종교적인 이유는 무엇일까요?
8. 신이 존재하나요? 그렇다면 신은 비종교적인 사람보다 종교적인 사람들은 더 좋아하나요? 왜 그렇게 생각하는지 말하세요.
9. 인간은 사후에 천국을 가기 위해 교회를 다녀야 하나요, 아니면 그건 상관이 없나요? 왜 그렇게 생각하는지 말하세요.
10. 사람이 죽은 후에 어떤 일이 생길까요? 왜 그렇게 생각하는지 말하세요.
   a. 사람들은 천국이나 지옥에 간다.
   b. 어떤 일도 생기지 않고 그냥 모든 것이 사라진다.